A LAYMAN'S LOVE OF LETTERS

Works by
George Macaulay Trevelyan, O.M.

ENGLISH SOCIAL HISTORY

ILLUSTRATED ENGLISH SOCIAL HISTORY
>   VOLUME I   *Chaucer's England and the Early Tudors*
>   VOLUME II   *The Age of Shakespeare and the Stuart Period*
>   VOLUME III   *The Eighteenth Century*
>   VOLUME IV   *The Nineteenth Century*

HISTORY OF ENGLAND

BRITISH HISTORY IN THE NINETEENTH
>   CENTURY AND AFTER (1782–1919)

ENGLAND UNDER QUEEN ANNE:
>   *Blenheim*
>   *Ramillies and the Union with Scotland*
>   *The Peace and the Protestant Succession*

ENGLAND IN THE AGE OF WYCLIFFE

GREY OF FALLODON

GARIBALDI'S DEFENCE OF THE ROMAN REPUBLIC

GARIBALDI AND THE THOUSAND

GARIBALDI AND THE MAKING OF ITALY

LORD GREY OF THE REFORM BILL, THE LIFE OF
>   CHARLES, SECOND EARL OF GREY

CLIO, A MUSE, AND OTHER ESSAYS

AN AUTOBIOGRAPHY AND OTHER ESSAYS

CARLYLE: AN ANTHOLOGY

A LAYMAN'S
LOVE OF LETTERS

BEING THE
CLARK LECTURES
DELIVERED AT CAMBRIDGE
OCTOBER–NOVEMBER 1953

BY

G. M. TREVELYAN, O.M.

Master of Trinity College, 1940–1951
Formerly Regius Professor of Modern
History in the University of Cambridge

LONGMANS, GREEN AND CO
LONDON · NEW YORK · TORONTO

LONGMANS, GREEN AND CO LTD
6 & 7 CLIFFORD STREET LONDON W I
ALSO AT MELBOURNE AND CAPE TOWN

LONGMANS, GREEN AND CO INC
55 FIFTH AVENUE NEW YORK 3

LONGMANS, GREEN AND CO
215 VICTORIA STREET TORONTO I

ORIENT LONGMANS LTD
BOMBAY CALCUTTA MADRAS

First published 1954

PRINTED IN GREAT BRITAIN BY
SPOTTISWOODE, BALLANTYNE AND CO. LTD.
LONDON AND COLCHESTER

Contents

ACKNOWLEDGMENTS

Acknowledgments for permission to include copyright material are due to the following:—

Mrs. George Bambridge, Messrs. Macmillan & Co. Ltd., and Messrs. Doubleday & Co. Inc. for *The Harp Song of the Dane Women* from *"Puck of Pook's Hill"* by Rudyard Kipling (copyright 1906 by Rudyard Kipling); Messrs. Jonathan Cape Ltd., and Messrs. Henry Holt & Co. Inc. for *On Wenlock Edge* from *"A Shropshire Lad"* by A. E. Housman, and *Tell Me Not Here* from *"Last Poems"* by A. E. Housman (copyright, 1922, by Henry Holt & Co. Inc.; copyright, 1950, by Barclays Bank Ltd.); Messrs. Constable & Co. Ltd. for extracts from *Poetical Works of George Meredith*; Miss Margaret Cropper for *The Grey Ewe* from *"The End of the Road"* published by Messrs. Thomas Nelson & Sons Ltd.; Mr. E. M. Forster for material from *Aspects of the Novel* published by Messrs. Edward Arnold & Co.; Messrs. Methuen & Co. Ltd. for quotations from *Collected Poems* by G. W. Young; and the Editor of *The Sunday Times* for material from an article of September 14th, 1952.

I

Yes, you may well wonder to see me standing up behind the desk. I have often taken the chair at the Clark Lectures, while we absorbed instruction and inhaled delight from discourses at once learned and inspiring, delivered by men whose life's work was the study of English literature. For this purpose I am only a layman—a "lewed man" as Chaucer would call me—not a professional scholar or critic at all. Perhaps those who are responsible for thus intruding me upon you wish to remind the University that the Clark Lectures are provided by Trinity; it is not unnatural that the Council should job an old servant of the College into this place. None the less I was surprised and taken aback by their invitation, for my lectures cannot have the kind of merit and authority to which you are accustomed on these occasions.

All the same, here I am; I have yielded to the temptation of hearing again, in the words of Walt Whitman, "the clear glad sound of my own voice". I am indeed only an historian, but I have always held that History and Literature are sisters, and that their complete separation is unnatural and injurious. (Incidentally, I am glad to think that the English Tripos is conducted very largely on that principle.) Moreover, it is perhaps well that for one year the Clark Lectures should represent a lay point of view—I do not say *the* lay point of view, for my thesis is that there ought to be many such. *Quot homines, tot sententiae.*

I shall begin by stating first my own deep debt of gratitude to professional scholars and critics of English letters; and, second, my reasons for thinking that the existence of schools of English at the Universities is of special value in our present state of society.

First as to my personal debt. If I start counting from my

nursery days of rapturous devotion to Scott's and Macaulay's Lays at the age of six, I have now for seventy-two years lived and had my being in English literature, particularly English poetry. But my understanding of our poets and prose writers has been increased and my love of them maintained by the comment of professional critics.

Andrew Bradley, Walter Raleigh, Granville Barker, besides others whom we still have with us, have prevented me from ever feeling that I had exhausted the joys of Shakespeare, though I must have read his greatest plays some seventy times. Custom might stale even Hamlet's infinite variety at the seventieth reading, if the reader's zest were not renewed by the learned comments of first-rate modern minds.

I heard many years ago a witty rhyme which has remained in my head ever since. I don't know who wrote it or whether it has ever been in print. It runs as follows:

> I dreamt last night that Shakespeare's ghost
> Sat for a civil service post.
> The subject chosen for the year
> Was taken from the play *King Lear*.
> And Shakespeare did it very badly,
> Because he had not read his Bradley.

I hope you have all read your Bradley on the Four Great Tragedies. I have often. It is a splendid aid to Shakespeare in the study, and Granville Barker has added to it a necessary complement, in some respects a criticism, by dealing with Shakespeare on the stage.

And what a sure guide to the nature of Hardy's novels, their strength and their weakness, do we find in Lord David Cecil's Clark Lectures for 1942—and what a stimulus to read the best of them again at once! And how excellent is his more recent volume, called *Poets and Story Tellers*! At one time I thought that I admired Milton's poetry more than Mr. T. S. Eliot admired it. But since the publication of his Annual Lecture on a *Master Mind* in the *Proceedings of the British Academy* for 1947, I have found my perception of the distinctive merits of *Paradise Lost* still further increased by that just and powerful analysis. I am proud to think that my own beloved friend John Bailey, one of the galaxy of leader-writers for *The Times Literary Supplement* under Bruce Richmond, dedicated to me in 1923 his volume entitled *The Continuity of Letters*, a noble vindication of the theme implied in that title.

Or again, let us take examples from our Cambridge School of English. Verrall came over from his classical studies to fill the Chair of English Literature as its first occupant. That was in 1911, which proved unhappily to be the year before his death; but dying, he bequeathed us a handful of gold. His analysis of the prose structure of Meg Merrilies' curse—

Ride your ways Ellangowan!

is indeed a subtle and enlightening piece of criticism that should send unbelievers in Scott to search *Guy Mannering*. And indeed I am sorry for those who, because Sir Walter's pattern English is not up to the level of his native woodnotes wild, find that they must forgo the company of Meg Merrilies, Dandie Dinmont, Dirk Hatterick, Dominie Sampson and the lawyer Pleydell—all in that one great novel. (Verrall's *Literary Essays, Classical and Modern*, 1913, pp. 248–64.)

And at the present time, when so much good work is being done by our now full-grown English School, Professor Basil Willey, in the last chapter of his *Seventeenth Century Background*, entitled "Wordsworth and the Locke Tradition" has shown how Wordsworth was in the higher reaches of thought a child of that earlier epoch, though a very unusual child certainly. These are a few examples, which could be indefinitely multiplied, of the way in which the professional scholar and critic can help the layman like myself who reads only for pleasure "with his feet on the fender"—or ought one nowadays to say "with his feet at the stove"?

So much for my personal gratitude. But, as I said just now, the study of English at our Universities is indispensable in the present state of society, which is very different as a patron of

Letters from what it was sixty years ago. At that time the study
of our national heritage in poetry and prose flourished on a
broad economic and social basis, which stood in relatively little
need of help from an endowed school of English at the Universities. And this for a number of reasons.

In the first place, a larger amount of literary criticism was
supplied by newspapers and periodicals—employing for that
purpose many scholars and literary men, who could not have
balanced their family budgets merely on the sale of the
books they wrote. It therefore mattered less that there was
but scant endowment for scholars of English literature at the
Universities.

In those days many more papers catered for their middle-
class clientele by serious reviewing. I do not say that it was
better in quality than present-day reviewing, but it was certainly greater in quantity. There was no difficulty then about
newsprint, and the best weekly papers could expatiate at large,
without being unwillingly compelled to keep critics of the
eminence of Desmond MacCarthy to the limit of a thousand
words or less. Fairly long reviews of books appeared even in
daily and evening papers, some of which have since disappeared
like the *Westminster Gazette*, the *Pall Mall*, the *St. James's
Gazette*, the *Globe*, the *Standard* and the *Morning Post*, while
some others still extant have ceased to notice books. The
deceased *Athenæum* was essentially academic in outlook. And
there were long reviews not only in the weeklies but in the
quarterlies and monthlies. In this way was literature kept before
the nation's eyes, and discussed very fully in public from various
points of view, no longer under the dangerous monopoly and
tyranny of the pre-Victorian *Edinburgh* and *Quarterly* Reviews;
and moreover, as I have said, great numbers of literary
scholars and critics could make a livelihood by reviewing for
the Press.

Secondly there were more and larger private libraries.
Many people could then afford to buy books, and they lived
not in flats but in houses with space for bookshelves. It is indeed
true that there are now more public libraries, and let us be

very thankful for that. But reading the English authors at home in the evening was more customary, and much was gained both in pleasure and profit by reading in a well-stocked library chosen by oneself, jumping up from the perusal of A's book to look out something it suggests in B's book, or in the *Dictionary of National Biography*. It is an ideal that can more seldom be realized today.

At Cambridge the College Libraries were indeed less well adapted than they now are for the needs of students; but undergraduates then had more books in their own rooms. From the point of view of Tripos work the College and Faculty libraries go far to fill the gap, but for the personal and private enjoyment of English literature the undergraduates' own book-shelves were more serviceable when they were larger and better filled.

One not very important but very significant custom was that of giving profusely, as school prizes, well-bound copies of the standard English poets and prose writers. I came up to Cambridge in 1893 with a large and well-loved collection acquired in that way. Schools cannot now afford to patronize literature on that sort of scale.

But, you may say, the boys didn't read their prizes. Well, some did and others didn't. All at least had the chance. And the same may be said of their parents sitting at home among their long shelves of books.

Then again there was more leisure. Very large professional and middle classes could then afford and find houses and domestic servants to run them; therefore they enjoyed far more leisure than their successors, male and especially female, who must clean their own flats, and cook their own food. And since there was not the competition of cinema, wireless and television, much of that large leisure was spent in reading books.

Then again education, secondary and higher, was more favourable to literature, because science had not then made such deep invasion. With a knowledge of the Bible stories more or less universal, and of the Classical myths very general

among schoolboys, English literature with its constant allusions
to the Bible and the Classics was more easily understood and
appreciated. In general the whole background and atmosphere of thought and knowledge was more literary than today.
There was less specialization and more culture.

The era of which I am speaking was the period of my own
boyhood and youth, the last two decades of the Nineteenth
Century and the first decade of this. In the early years of that
era, Carlyle and Ruskin, Browning and Tennyson were still
alive, and though they were past producing any more good
work, the best they had written in earlier years was still being
read, and they themselves were well known as national figures,
and revered as glories of our nation. Meanwhile the younger
authors who were then writing much of their best work,
included Stevenson, Hardy, Meredith, Henry James, Leslie
Stephen, Walter Pater, Kipling, Samuel Butler, Barrie, Shaw,
Wells, Chesterton, Robert Bridges, Conrad, Galsworthy,
Arnold Bennett, Richard Jefferies, W. H. Hudson, John
Morley, Mrs. Humphry Ward, A. E. Housman, E. M. Forster,
Yeats, Synge, George Moore, Conan Doyle and others—and
critics like A. C. Bradley and Raleigh and Birrell. Partly,
perhaps, because so many remarkable writers were among us,
partly from the over-hang of an older tradition, I think there
was a very widespread interest in our literary heritage, firmly
based on prevalent economic and social circumstances, without
much needing the aid of a school of English at the Universities. Well, times have changed.

In the 'nineties I lived here among a literary set of undergraduates. I doubt if we should any of us have chosen to do the
English Tripos even if it had existed. At any rate we were all
studying other subjects with ardour. But we had time and
devotion left over to be constantly reading and talking about
poetry. Indeed I was discovering for myself George Meredith
as a poet—it was a discovery then, though he was already
famous as a novelist. I recollect, with some shame now for our
youthful error, that we were unfriendly to the idea of an
English Tripos, which was then being talked about as possible

in the future. We thought it would be "low", a degradation of English literature to make it an examination subject. Our goddess, poetry, could look after herself and her worshippers without the mediation of priests. Great heavens, how were you to lecture and examine on Shelley's *Arethusa*, Browning's *Saul*, or Meredith's *Hymn to Colour*? Such was then our layman's pride. It was not that we thought too little of English literature, but that we thought it too sacred. We were wrong of course. As time went on I modified my opinion, and when in 1911 our adored Verrall became the first Professor of English Literature at Cambridge, I changed it altogether.

Time will not turn back. The present state of things, as I have described it, will continue. Indeed it is possible that the country may become even poorer than it is now, and it is probable that what wealth it has will be yet more evenly distributed. In that case the more expensive newspapers, weekly and daily, who still do serious reviewing are likely to disappear, if fewer people can afford to buy them, and we shall be left with nothing but the cheap Press. Were that to occur the tradition and study of English literature might almost disappear, if it had no fastness in the Universities, those free institutions for which, I am glad to say, the modern British State has a generous kindness of a truly liberal sort.

For these reasons, though a layman, I am all for an endowed priesthood, provided there are no articles for the clergy to sign, and no dogmas for them to impose upon us. And above all I object to excommunication ("debunking") of great writers of the past on some modern theory, or to suit some phase of thought and feeling, which like all phases of thought and feeling will itself pass away. What reason is there to think that Twentieth-century taste in literature is any better than that of the Nineteenth Century and of the Eighteenth Century, both of which we have in turn discarded, or at least very widely enlarged? Let each reader discover by experiment what are his own tastes, irrespective of the fashion of the hour.

I would suggest this formula: any author who was for a number of years together, considered to be a great writer by a large number of the elect spirits of any former age, must have some great merit, and if changes of fashion in thought, and in literary taste, now make that merit less obvious, it is none the less there: it is to be sought, or at least it is not to be denied without seeking.

The whole field of literature is open to us all, for each one of us to make his individual choice. We shall not all of us care equally for the same things, and for heaven's sake let us not try to coerce our brother by telling him he must not read, or ought not to enjoy, the debunkee of the hour, whether it be Scott, Carlyle, Swinburne, Browning or Kipling. Your brother whom you take to task may know less about literature than you do, and yet he may be sensitive to something really good to which you happen to be blind. We all of us have blind spots in our love of literature; certainly I have. And, what is more, even great literary critics often have had such blind spots. Sometimes indeed they do very great service, as when Dryden first made the world aware of the supreme merit of Shakespeare and Milton. But think of Dr. Johnson's condemnation of *Lycidas* and Gray's poetry. And note the errors of Matthew Arnold, who I suppose did more than anyone else to teach criticism and good taste in letters. He showed readers what to look for in poetry and in prose, what kind of standards to apply. Later critics have stood upon his shoulders, and therefore some of them enjoy a wider view than his. But, great critic though he was, I do not think his actual choices were always right.

For instance, what he said about Byron and about Shelley was valuable, and yet we may disagree with his conclusion as to their relative merits. I cannot help suspecting that he was unable to feel to the full the rare beauty of Shelley's very best lyrics, or he could not have ranked him below Byron as a poet.

While I say this I must add that in the main I agree with the criticism he made in 1888 of Dowden's *Life of Shelley*, and his reaction against the excessive adulation of Shelley regarded as a responsible member of society. Peacock, who had known Shelley well, had said, in *Fraser's Magazine*, much the same thing on that score thirty years before Arnold. Or turn to the wisdom of Walter Bagehot. He was not only a layman but that essence of a layman—a banker! Yet he had written, as early as 1856, an excellent appreciation both of Shelley's poetry and of his life—in the second volume of Bagehot's collected works you can find the essay, sandwiched in between one on "The Character of Sir Robert Peel" and one on "The Crédit mobilier and Banking companies in France"! As regards the character of Shelley, so very different from that of Sir Robert Peel, he wrote some words which seem to me as good as the remarks which Matthew Arnold passed on the same subject a generation later.

> This strange story [writes Bagehot], is in various ways illustrative of Shelley's character. It shows the impulsive temperament, not definitely intending evil, is hurried forward, so to say, *over* actions and crimes which would seem to indicate depravity—which would do so in ordinary human nature, but which do not indicate in it anything like the same degree of guilt. Driven by singular passion across a tainted region, it retains no taint; on a sudden it passes through evil, but preserves its purity. So curious is this character, that a record of its actions may read like a libel on its life.

Bravo banker!

I now come to what Arnold wrote about Byron, in *Essays in Criticism* (II. 202–4). I will read his summing up in full, and then will most respectfully comment upon it.

> His own aristocratic class, whose cynical make-believe drove him to fury; the great middle-class, on whose impregnable Philistinism he shattered himself to pieces—how little have either of these felt Byron's vital influence! As the inevitable break-up of the old order comes, as the English middle-class slowly awakens from its intellectual sleep of two centuries, as our actual present world, to which this sleep has condemned us, shows itself more clearly,— our world of an aristocracy materialised and null, a middle-class purblind and hideous, a lower class crude and brutal—we shall turn our eyes again, and to more purpose, upon this passionate and dauntless soldier of a forlorn hope, who, ignorant of the future and unconsoled by its promises, nevertheless waged against the conservation of the old impossible world so fiery battle; waged

it till he fell—waged it with such splendid and imperishable excellence of sincerity and strength.

Wordworth's value is of another kind. Wordsworth has an insight into permanent sources of joy and consolation for mankind which Byron has not; his poetry gives us more which we may rest upon than Byron's—more which we can rest upon now, and which men may rest upon always. I place Wordsworth's poetry, therefore, above Byron's on the whole, although in some points he was greatly Byron's inferior, and although Byron's poetry will always, probably, find more readers than Wordsworth's, and will give pleasure more easily. But these two, Wordsworth and Byron, stand, it seems to me, first and pre-eminent in actual performance, a glorious pair, among the English poets of this century. Keats had probably, indeed, a more consummate poetic gift than either of them; but he died having produced too little and being as yet too immature to rival them. I for my part can never even think of equalling with them any other of their contemporaries—either Coleridge, poet and philosopher wrecked in a mist of opium; or Shelley, beautiful and ineffectual angel, beating in the void his luminous wings in vain. Wordsworth and Byron stand out by themselves. When the year 1900 is turned, and our nation comes to recount her poetic glories in the century which has then just ended, the first names with her will be these.

Such is the great critic's opinion. It seems to me an excellent account of Byron's value; but, much as I admire and enjoy the last half of *Childe Harold*, *The Vision of Judgment* and much of *Don Juan*, I cannot find in them or anywhere in Byron enough of first-rate poetical quality to place him above, or even in the same class as, Shelley, Coleridge and Keats.

The satire in Byron's *Vision of Judgment* is very good, yet even as satire I am not sure that it has the artistic perfection of Dryden's *Absalom and Achitophel*.

Prig that I am, to go on talking about Byron in this way! Listen to this jingle of his and love him for it, thinking of Missolonghi.

> When a man has no freedom to fight for at home,
>   Let him combat for that of his neighbours;
> Let him think of the glories of Greece and of Rome,
>   And get knocked on his head for his labours.

> To do good to mankind is the chivalrous plan,
>> And is always as nobly requited;
> Then battle for freedom wherever you can,
>> And, if not shot or hanged, you'll be knighted.

Yet all that sort of gallant fun, of which there is such plenty, and even his noblest note:

> Yet, freedom, yet thy banner torn but flying
> Streams like a thunder-storm *against* the wind

and his picture of the ball in Brussels before Waterloo, and his tales in verse which Scott despaired to rival in the public favour—all these together do not seem to me to belong to the order of Keats' Odes, Shelley's *Cloud* and *West Wind*, Coleridge's *Ancient Mariner* and *Kubla Khan*, or Matthew Arnold's own *Thyrsis*.

Apart from what he most justly says of Wordsworth, Arnold in the passage I have quoted seems to me to be judging poets too much by their merit as political and social reformers. To quote his own *Last Word* to a radical friend:

> Charge once more, then, and be dumb!
> Let the victors, when they come,
> When the forts of folly fall
> Find thy body near the wall!

Very well said. But leading a forlorn hope does not mean that a man is a supreme poet. Byron's attack on the Anti-Jacobin world of his day was a spirited action; but now that Anti-Jacobinism has for a hundred years been as dead as Lord Eldon, can Byron's defiance of it signify quite so much to the world as once it did! Our political, social and intellectual troubles are of a different character from what they were in the days of the Luddites, Peterloo and Queen Caroline. We must judge Byron now by his poetic quality. His attack on the society of his day has historic interest as well as intrinsic value as literature, but the subject is not of the same perennial order of importance as the truth of beauty, that we find not only in Wordsworth, but in Keats and Shelley. It is the beauty of poetry that is of everlasting value, not its social use, or even

2

its intellectual content, except in so far as that content takes the shape of beauty.

I may indeed be in error. But it is not intrinsically impossible that Matthew Arnold was mistaken. "The worst of great thinkers is they so often think wrong." But their words are well worthy of your consideration. And so too with the views of modern professional critics. They have much to say that is of value to you, but probably each of them has his blind spot. The wisest man is wrong about something. That is true alike in the spheres of politics, life and letters. Seek the advice you think best, but trust no man's opinion absolutely about everything. And, in any case, what you yourself can really feel in appreciation of poetry or prose, is worth more to *you* than what you are told by authority, or (not necessarily the same thing) by the fashion of your own contemporaries. We are each of us different one from another and each has potentially a different response to literature.

Rightly or wrongly Arnold thought that the massive volume of Byron's work weighed more in the everlasting scales than what either Shelley or Keats has left us. Yet in spite of such high authority, I still agree with the three laymen of Trinity (Arthur Hallam, Monckton Milnes and Sunderland), who in 1829 went over to the Union at Oxford to maintain the then astonishing paradox that Shelley was a greater poet than Byron. And I note in passing that in that same epoch, Trinity undergraduates and B.A.s (laymen all) did much to propagate the belief that Wordsworth was a great poet, in a world that was just ready to receive that novel doctrine.

In taking up a position contrary to so famous a critic as Arnold, I feel that I ought to justify myself in your ears by quoting from the poets whose relative merit is the question.

I will begin by quoting verses from Byron at his very best:

> The isles of Greece! the isles of Greece!
>   Where burning Sappho loved and sung,
> Where grew the arts of war and peace,
>   Where Delos rose and Phoebus sprung!
> Eternal summer gilds them yet,
> But all, except their sun, is set.

The mountains look on Marathon—
　And Marathon looks on the sea;
And musing there an hour alone,
　I dream'd that Greece might still be free;
For, standing on the Persians' grave,
I could not deem myself a slave.

A king sat on the rocky brow
　Which looks o'er sea-born Salamis;
And ships, by thousands, lay below,
　And men in nations;—all were his!
He counted them at break of day—
And when the sun set where were they?

Must *we* but weep o'er days more blest?
　Must *we* but blush?—Our fathers bled.
Earth! render back from out thy breast
　A remnant of our Spartan dead!
Of the three hundred grant but three,
To make a new Thermopylae!

Trust not for freedom to the Franks—
　They have a king who buys and sells:
In native swords and native ranks,
　The only hope of courage dwells;
But Turkish force and Latin fraud
Would break your shield, however broad.

Fill high the bowl with Samian wine!
　Our virgins dance beneath the shade—
I see their glorious black eyes shine;
　But, gazing on each glowing maid,
My own the burning tear-drop laves,
To think such breasts must suckle slaves

Place me on Sunium's marbled steep,
　Where nothing, save the waves and I
May hear our mutual murmurs sweep:
　There, swan-like, let me sing and die
A land of slaves shall ne'er be mine—
Dash down yon cup of Samian wine!

I should be less disinclined to approve Arnold's award of the apple, in his judgment of Paris between Byron, Shelley and Keats, if any large part of Byron's political, satirical and narrative poems were on a level with the verses I have just read. But the *Isles of Greece* is a thing unique. Byron stuck it into the Third Canto of *Don Juan*, where it shines on an alien background, a star of singular irrelevance.

Then again, in a different mood, we have from him:

> There be none of Beauty's daughters
>   With a magic like thee;
> And like music on the waters
>   Is thy sweet voice to me:
> When, as if its sound were causing
> The charmed ocean's pausing,
> The waves lie still and gleaming,
> And the lull'd winds seem dreaming:
>
> And the midnight moon is weaving
>   Her bright chain o'er the deep;
> Whose breast is gently heaving,
>   As an infant's asleep:
> So the spirit bows before thee,
> To listen and adore thee;
> With a full but soft emotion,
> Like the swell of summer's ocean.

If Byron had written many more short lyrics as good as

> There be none of Beauty's daughters

they might be compared to Shelley's many fragments of similar length. But it seems to me to occupy rather a solitary position in Byron's large volume. As to Shelley's fragments there are scores of them of similar or higher quality. I will take a few at random. Here are five little pieces from a single page in my Shelley:

> Music, when soft voices die,
> Vibrates in the memory—
> Odours, when sweet violets sicken,
> Live within the sense they quicken.

Rose leaves, when the rose is dead,
Are heaped for the beloved's bed;
And so thy thoughts, when thou art gone,
Love itself shall slumber on.

Unfathomable Sea! whose waves are years,
  Ocean of Time, whose waters of deep woe
Are brackish with the salt of human tears!
    Thou shoreless flood, which in thy ebb and flow
Claspest the limits of mortality!
And sick of prey, yet howling on for more,
Vomitest thy wrecks on its inhospitable shore,
Treacherous in calm, and terrible in storm,
      Who shall put forth on thee,
      Unfathomable Sea?

  A widow bird sate mourning for her love
      Upon a wintry bough;
  The frozen wind crept on above,
      The freezing stream below.

There was no leaf upon the forest bare,
      No flower upon the ground,
And little motion in the air
      Except the mill-wheel's sound.

Tell me thou star, whose wings of light
Speed thee in thy fiery flight,
In what cavern of the night
      Will thy pinions close now?

Tell me moon, thou pale and grey
Pilgrim of heaven's homeless way,
In what depth of night or day
      Seekest thou repose now?

Weary wind who wanderest
Like the world's rejected guest,
Hast thou still some secret nest
      On the tree or billow?

> Rough wind, that moanest loud
>   Grief too sad for song;
> Wild wind, when sullen cloud
>   Knells all the night long;
> Sad storm, whose tears are vain,
> Bare woods, whose branches stain,
> Deep caves and dreary main,
>   Wail for the world's wrong!

And take from *Prometheus Unbound* this bit of mysticism exalted into the sphere of vision and music.

> Life of Life! thy lips enkindle
>   With their love the breath between them;
> And thy smiles before they dwindle
>   Make the cold air fire; then screen them
> In those locks, where whoso gazes
> Faints, entangled in their mazes.
>
> Child of Light! thy limbs are burning
>   Through the vest which seems to hide them;
> As the radiant lines of morning
>   Through the clouds ere they divide them;
> And this atmosphere divinest
> Shrouds thee whereso'er thou shinest.
>
> Fair are others; none beholds thee,
>   But thy voice sounds low and tender
> Like the fairest, for it folds thee
>   From the sight, that liquid splendour,
> And all feel, yet see thee never,
> As I feel now, lost for ever!
>
> Lamp of earth! where'er thou movest
>   Its dim shapes are clad with brightness,
> And the souls of whom thou lovest
>   Walk upon the winds with lightness,
> Till they fail, as I am failing,
> Dizzy, lost, yet unbewailing!

What does it mean, do you ask? I answer in Housman's words: 'Blake again and again, as Shakespeare now and then, gives us poetry neat or unadulterated with so little meaning that nothing except poetic emotion is perceived and matters.' And so with Shelley here.

And besides such fragments, scattered throughout Shelley's pages thick as stars in the Milky Way, there are complete poems of moderate length, like *The Cloud*, *The West Wind*, *The Skylark*, *Arethusa*, maintained throughout their length at a supreme height of poetry. They are too long to quote, but take this also, a complete poem:

> Swiftly walk over the western wave
> > Spirit of Night!
> Out of the misty eastern cave,
> Where, all the long and lone daylight,
> Thou wovest dreams of joy and fear,
> Which make thee terrible and dear,—
> > Swift be thy flight!
>
> Wrap thy form in a mantle grey,
> > Star-inwrought!
> Blind with thine hair the eyes of day,
> Kiss her until she be wearied out,
> Then wander o'er city, and sea, and land,
> Touching all with thine opiate wand—
> > Come, long sought!
>
> When I arose and saw the dawn,
> > I sighed for thee;
> When light rode high, and the dew was gone,
> And noon lay heavy on flower and tree,
> And the weary Day turned to his rest,
> Lingering like an unloved guest,
> > I sighed for thee.
>
> Thy brother Death came, and cried,
> > Wouldst thou me?
> Thy sweet child Sleep, the filmy-eyed,
> > Murmured like a noontide bee,
> Shall I nestle by thy side?
> Wouldst thou me?—And I replied,
> > No, not thee!

> Death will come when thou art dead,
>   Soon, too soon—
> Sleep will come when thou art fled;
> Of neither would I ask the boon
> I ask of thee, beloved Night—
> Swift be thine approaching flight.
>   Come soon, soon!

There is a story of which I am very fond (though I don't know whether it is authentic), to the effect that Shelley's two sisters lived to be admirers of Alfred Tennyson's early poems. "Yes," said the dear old ladies, "young Mr. Tennyson writes very well. But he doesn't write as well as our Bysshe."

I agree with Matthew Arnold that Shelley was "a beautiful but ineffectual angel", etc., etc., as regards his system of philosophic thought. But what of that? He was not ineffectual as a lyric poet, in which capacity he stands in the very first rank, and that is what matters.

And then there is Keats, whom also Matthew Arnold placed below Byron, because he had written so little owing to his premature death. Perhaps the great critic is inclined for once to give a little too much to quantity and not enough to quality. And after all Keats has left us a good deal of the very best. I have not time to quote *Hyperion*, or the three great Odes, on *A Nightingale*, *A Grecian Urn* and *Psyche*, but take the short poem entitled *Written on May Day*.

> Mother of Hermes! and still youthful Maia!
>   May I sing to thee
> As thou wast hymned on the shores of Baiae?
>   Or may I woo thee
> In earlier Sicilian? or thy smiles
> Seek as they once were sought, in Grecian isles,
> By bards who died content on pleasant sward,
> Leaving great verse unto a little clan?
> O, give me their old vigour, and unheard
> Save of the quiet Primrose, and the span
>   Of heaven and few ears,
> Rounded by thee, my song should die away
>   Content as theirs,
> Rich in the simple worship of a day.

And the following sonnet has an almost unbearable pathos, in view of what actually happened to Keats:

> When I have fears that I may cease to be
>   Before my pen has glean'd my teeming brain
> Before high-piled books, in charact'ry,
>   Hold like rich garners the full-ripen'd grain;
> When I behold, upon the night's starr'd face,
>   Huge cloudy symbols of a high romance,
> And think that I may never live to trace
>   Their shadows, with the magic hand of chance;
> And when I feel, fair creature of an hour!
>   That I shall never look upon thee more,
> Never have relish in the faery power
>   Of unreflecting love!—then on the shore
> Of the wide world I stand alone, and think,
> Till Love and Fame to nothingness do sink.

This is surely, to use Matthew Arnold's own words on another matter, "than Byron's woe more tragic far". There is here no "pageant of a bleeding heart", but the sad solitary thought of one who died at Rome in the mistaken belief that "his name was writ in water".

Last of all, we come to Coleridge, whom also Matthew Arnold bids us to place below Byron as a poet. His reason for this decision I have already told you; it is that Coleridge was "a poet and philosopher wrecked in a mist of opium". That is all he says on the matter. Now let us examine that dictum more carefully. It may or may not be true as a description of the life and work of Coleridge in the Nineteenth Century. With that I am not here concerned. But it seems to me wholly false as an account of the work of Coleridge as a poet in the last four years of the Eighteenth Century. Between 1797 and 1800 he wrote poems which seem to me better than any-thing Byron ever wrote—*Kubla Khan*, *The Ancient Mariner*, the First Part of *Christabel* (the Second Part is a little later and much less good), and *Frost at Midnight*. There is other fine work of his belonging to the same brief period, but I name these poems as placing him very high indeed among our

English poets, certainly above Byron. One of the many curious things about Coleridge is that he did not know how good his best poems were: well we have found that out for him.

Now my point against Matthew Arnold is this, that the best poems of Coleridge show no sign of being "lost in a mist of opium". I set aside the question whether or not *Kubla Khan* (1797) was composed under the influence of the "anodyne" which, as he says in his note of 1816, he had taken before the lines came into his head. My point is that in any case *Kubla Khan* as we now have it is a perfect poem, complete and consistent in itself (whether or not there were more lines composed which were driven out of his head by a visitor from Porlock, as he asserted twenty years later). Mr. Humphry House, in his important Clark Lectures for 1951–2 on the subject of Coleridge, has encouraged us by cogent argument and analysis to think *Kubla Khan* a perfect poem, a self-consistent whole with no loose ends about it. As to its being "lost in a mist of opium", no description could be further from the truth, either about *Kubla Khan*, the *Ancient Mariner*, *Christabel I*, *Frost at Midnight* or the Mont Blanc hymn. There is nothing "misty" about any of them. Their language, their story, their images are as clear as they are forcible, original and lovely. One sentence in the strange preface to *Kubla Khan* which its author wrote twenty years later can be accepted without demur, his account of its composition—'if that indeed can be called composition in which all the images rose up as things with a parallel production of the corresponding expressions, without any sensation or consciousness of effort'. The work so accomplished may or may not have been in part the inspiration of opium, but it is as far as possible from being "lost in a mist of opium". The whole poem has a marvellous clarity of vision and of expression. The fact is that in those great years 1797 to 1800 Coleridge was at the height of his undimmed powers, creating very great and singularly faultless poems, and being himself, until his return from Germany, a fairly healthy man, not unvisited by that sense of joy of which he had soon to bemoan the loss as the Nineteenth Century dawned. So, in spite of

Matthew Arnold, I place not only Wordsworth, but Shelley, Keats and Coleridge above Byron, as poets.

Another particular judgment of Matthew Arnold's from which I respectfully differ, is his dictum that *The Elegy written in a country churchyard* was not Gray's best poem. You will find what he says in Ward's *English Poets*, five volumes which still remain one of the best collections of our national heritage in poetry, with a number of admirable introductions to each poet. Arnold writes:

> Gray himself maintained that the *Elegy* was not his best work in poetry, and he was right. High as is the praise due to the *Elegy*, it is yet true that in other productions of Gray he exhibits poetical qualities even higher than those exhibited in the *Elegy*.

Now twenty-five pages back in the same volume of Ward's *Poets*, Swinburne, no mean critic, had written precisely the opposite in his introduction to Collins:

> As an elegiac poet [writes Swinburne] Gray holds for all ages to come his unassailable and sovereign station; as a lyric poet, he is simply unworthy to sit at the feet of Collins. Whether it may not be a greater thing than ever was done by the greater lyrist, to have written a poem of such high perfection and such universal appeal to the tenderest and noblest depths of human feeling as Gray's *Elegy*, is of course another and wholly irrelevant question. But it is not a question which admits of debate at all, among men qualified to speak in such matters, that as a lyric poet Gray was not worthy to unloose the latchets of Collins' shoes.

For my part I agree with Swinburne on this particular issue. I think Gray's *Elegy* was his best work, and Collins' *Ode to Evening* a finer lyric poem than any of Gray's lyrics as distinct from his *Elegy*. But I do not follow Swinburne in saying that Matthew Arnold, because he thinks so highly of Gray's lyrics, is not "among men qualified to speak on such matters". That is a bit of red-headed exuberance.

I hope I have shown that you cannot be entirely guided in your particular choices by the opinion even of the most eminent critics, because, for one thing, they often differ from one another on matters of great moment. Critics, like us laymen, have their individual blind spots and their individual enthusiasms. Men are they. Listen to what critics say, but then choose for yourself. Critics will help you but do not let them hinder you. The response of your own ear, mind and heart to poetry is for you the ultimate criterion.

I take this occasion to record that George Meredith once said to me that he thought Matthew Arnold, if we take his poetry and prose together, was the most considerable writer of his age. I do not disagree. But his poetry, I think, has most to teach us now.

II

As my first lecture ended up on the heights, I propose to begin today by a sharp descent, discussing first a trivial adjunct of literature, the part, if any, that illustrations can play in volumes of poetry and of fiction.

For the highest flights of poetry I don't think illustrations can do anything except make the judicious swear. At those rare altitudes one resents pictures as an impertinence. Even engravings from Turner seem worse than irrelevant in Milton, and indeed the attempt to give pictorial definition to the vague and vasty deep of *Paradise Lost* goes right against the genius of the poem. The more realistic Dante, with his measurements of giants and his meetings with old acquaintances in hell, is more conceivable as a subject for the pencil, at any rate of a Botticelli. Even so I am glad that the brother Florentine's drawings of *The Divine Comedy* can be studied in a separate volume. I should not care to have them interleaved with the text.

There is, of course, William Blake. In his pages the poetry and the pictures (I will not insult them by calling them illustrations) have leapt together from his seething brain, and are twin aspects of a single great work of art.

Then there is the very different case of Samuel Rogers, not to my thinking a great poet at all. He craftily contrived for his book a certain immortality, by employing Turner and Stothard to do a series of most beautiful vignettes for his pages. They were the delight of my boyhood and I still look at them with great pleasure, though I do not read the poems among which they are set. They do not illustrate the book, they only adorn the volume.

Poetry, not quite of the first order, when it is of the narrative, romantic or ballad kind, is sometimes susceptible of real illustration. Gustave Doré found a subject suited to his romantic imagination in Tennyson's *Idylls of the King*. They cheer one up in the perusal of those narratives. But I hate to see Tennyson's finest lyrics, or his *Morte d'Arthur* illustrated—as was attempted in an unlucky hour by his pre-Raphaelite friends, in the edition of 1859. The element of narrative, whether in poetry or prose, is capable of bearing illustrations, if you can find an artist of real power whose nature is sympathetic to the spirit of the tale. George Cruikshank's work in *The Ingoldsby Legends* is an example. And I think he could have fitly illustrated much of Crabbe's poetry—the tale of Peter Grimes and his apprentices, for instance.

To sum up, the essence of poetry in its purer forms cannot be depicted. But narrative, whether in verse or prose, is more apt to bear illustration. And when we turn to prose fiction we enter a field wherein it is possible for an artist of genius to interpret to advantage the ideas of a novelist. It seldom happens, but it has happened. In the 'thirties and 'forties of the last century several great illustrators served novelists well. Of these the chief were George Cruikshank and H. K. Browne (who signed his work "Phiz"). And we must add to that brotherhood the unhappy Robert Seymour. These three men did much for Dickens by giving ocular reality to his incomparable menagerie of characters. By a lucky chance, the touch of the grotesque, of caricature, in the novelist was akin to the native spirit of his illustrators. H. B. or Tenniel, with their gentler art, could have done little for Dickens. But Seymour and "Phiz" helped him from the start, helped him to leap to fame as suddenly as Byron. The figure of Mr. Pickwick, as it arises in the mind's eye whenever his name is named, was first delineated in 1836 by Robert Seymour, who drew for the first numbers of *The Pickwick Papers* and then most tragically killed himself. "Phiz" took on dead Seymour's figure of Mr. Pickwick and multiplied it throughout the long remainder of the book, and himself created the outward semblance of Sam Weller, adding something of his own to the world's conception of Sam and his father. And in due course "Phiz" drew the images we know so well of Peggotty's household, David Copperfield's aunt,

ILLUSTRATION 25

Mr. Micawber and a hundred others in many of the novels. But the grim company in *Oliver Twist* is from the pencil of George Cruikshank himself: "Phiz" could never have done so well Bill Sikes and his dog or Fagin in the condemned cell.

No other great writer has been served by artists as Dickens was served by these men, though Surtees owes much to Leech for his figure of Jorrocks. Yes, Cruikshank and "Phiz" *served* Dickens, but they were themselves the leading partners in the work of lesser men such as Charles Lever and Harrison Ainsworth. Lever's *Charles O'Malley, Tom Burke of Ours* and *Jack Hinton* have little structure or merit as novels; they are a loose string of rollicking tales, mostly Irish, to me at least only readable in the original editions illustrated by "Phiz", who supplies a lively and amusing print for the crisis of each fresh adventure. I read round the illustrations and find it great fun.

This subordination of the author to the artist is even more marked in Harrison Ainsworth's *Windsor Castle, Tower of London, Guy Fawkes*, etc., where the macabre genius of Cruikshank has made a world of old cruelty and treachery spring alive into our sight and belief, rendering Ainsworth's text readable as comment on the pictures. My advice to you is never to read either Lever or Ainsworth except in the original illustrated editions, which very much more than double their value.

A finer work of literary imagination, *Alice*, has its great value enhanced by Tenniel's illustrations, which are now as much a part of our conception of Alice and her strange adventures as the pictures of "Phiz" are part of our idea of Dickens. One of the best deeds of the Victorians was the creation of children's books of real genius, equally dear to young and old. And illustrations are of the essence of their appeal. Beside *Alice* and before her in time, stands Thackeray's *Rose and the Ring*, set off by the sketches which he himself drew. Whether *Vanity Fair* gains or loses most by the author's own illustrations, *The Rose and the Ring* gains immensely. For Thackeray's weakness as a draughtsman does not matter in a comic setting, and how vividly he forces on our sight his own conception of Bulbo, the Gruffanuffs, and the rest of that memorable company.

To our own Cambridge climatures and countrymen there has recently been vouchsafed another example of a very witty book self-illustrated by the author, Mrs. Raverat's *Period Piece*. What, for instance, could be better as an explanation and enlargement of the text than the figure drawn of Mons. Cambon discoursing to the two *jeunes filles*, one of whom is taking mental notes to *do* him later in the day? That is *illustrating* a book, in the proper sense of the word. Of the large and still increasing class of works which we may define as "Victorian childhoods" Mrs. Raverat has done the masterpiece.

From illustration I pass to translation, a very important part of our literature. It is the only way in which some of us can have any knowledge at all of half the world's literature. In spite of the unwearied efforts of Professor Hill, there are still too few of us who can read the great Russian novels save in translations, and fortunately we have been well served in that respect. How much, even so, we lose, I cannot tell. But in the case of such great writers as Tolstoi and his peers, something must surely be lost even in the best translation. I know I should be sorry to read *Les dieux ont soif*, one of the world's best historical novels, in anything except the French of Anatole France, which is not its robe but its skin.

I fear I cannot read *Don Quixote* in Spanish. But the translation by Thomas Shelton is surely a fine work of literature, giving much of the value of the original, how much I know not. Now Shelton's translation of Cervantes was almost exactly contemporary with the authorized version of our Bible. The English language then had a pungency and a poetic power that it has since lost, in pursuit of scientific terms and journalistic phraseology. North's *Plutarch*, published in 1579, has passages which for sheer beauty of language vie with some of the scenes they suggested to Shakespeare for his *Anthony and Cleopatra*. Owing to its fortunate date in time, the greatest translation of all, the English Bible, was perhaps able to add to the value of the original as much as it lost. I cannot read Hebrew, but I can read the Greek of the New Testament and I do not think it is superior either in power or in poetic beauty to our translation. But the English language as we have developed it in our own time, though adequate for prose translation on a strictly prose level, is deficient in poetic quality.

It is indeed necessary for every well-educated man to read Homer in a translation if he does not know Greek, or Dante in a translation if he does not know Italian. And indeed there are many excellent translations, both in prose and verse, some of the best being done in our own day. Nevertheless in poetry of the highest order you cannot experience, even in the best of modern translations, that grip of the vitals, that disturbance of the whole being, which the *sound* of very great poetry alone can give.

Take, for example, a single line of Dante, the thirteenth line of the *Purgatorio*, where Dante, emerging from the infernal regions, has his eyes delighted with sight of the blue sky above him:

Dolce color d'oriental zaffiro

It means, being translated, "Sweet hue of orient sapphire." Yes, that is what it *means*. But those English words could never move me to tears, tears of pleasure in the sound of words, tears of gratitude for the beauty of the world in which we live, heaven above us, as do those four solemn, sweet Italian words:

Dolce color d'oriental zaffiro

They are of the same supreme order of poetry as Milton's moonlit waves of the sea:

> The sounds and seas, with all their finny drove
> Now to the moon in wavering morrice move.

Who could translate that in any language on earth without spilling its essence?

More than a year ago, in September 1952, I had an unpleasant surprise in turning over the *Sunday Times*. Mr.

Raymond Mortimer (for whose work as a critic of life and letters I have high respect) made an attack on Kipling so one-sided that it seemed to me to have lost the balance which we expect to find in serious criticism, and do find in Mr. Mortimer's customary work. Now, as I had the temerity in my first lecture to argue against positions taken up by Matthew Arnold, I shall be similarly courageous today in challenging an opinion of this eminent living critic, with most of whose opinions I am heartily in agreement, more often indeed than with Matthew Arnold's. It is not this time a question of the relative worth of great poets. We are now to move on a humbler level, not along the summits but round the slopes of the mountain of the Muses. And yet the issue is perhaps not unimportant, for it concerns the right of any lay lover of letters to enjoy the work of a famous author without being cast out of the literary synagogue.

I will first read to you the opening of Mr. Mortimer's article:

> Oh, no! we never mention him: his name is never heard. Kipling still has admirers, of course, who have been staunch for forty, fifty, sixty years. But to be re-read is one thing, to attract new readers quite another; and I wonder how many of his books are now in demand except as presents for children.
>
> When he is not forgotten, he is commonly disliked. One cause is his view of life, which was not far from Fascism. His contempt for educated Indians was silly and vulgar: he lowered our reputation in the sub-continent, and the evil that he did lives after him. He left India, it is true, at the age of twenty-seven, and knew little of the country outside Simla and the Punjab. Yet how could so inquisitive a man swallow—and retain—the prejudices of a suburban mem-sahib? The answer has often been given: he was a boy who never grew up. Throughout his writings, moreover, we find a morbid interest in cruelty. This seems to me nastier far than his political fanaticism, for which, I suspect, it was chiefly responsible [so writes Mr. Mortimer].

Is Kipling's name never to be heard? Why should we not "mention him"? I protest against this insinuation of the idea that it is bad form or "childish" to read and enjoy an author who was greatly admired (of course with reservations) by most of the best judges in his own time, because a debunking order has recently been issued.

To use the language of our day, I am not a "Kipling fan". But I enjoy reading most of his stories, and love many of them; of not a few I clearly see the faults. I differed from him in politics as much, I think, as Mr. Mortimer. So did my father and many Liberals of the Victorian and Edwardian days, who nevertheless took great pleasure in reading his stories as fast as they came out, while occasionally revolting against his crudities, political and other. I admit that we must recognize the strain of over-emphasis, of vulgarity, and occasionally of brutality that peeps through. Even when he was most in fashion half a century ago, there were always some people for whom his faults outweighed his merits. The youthful Max Beerbohm published during the Boer War a series of fierce cartoons entitled "Second Childhood of John Bull" (a rare volume that I possess and value); in it the protruding jaw of John Bull's favourite, Kipling, fared badly. But the Boer War is over long ago (tho' not I fear all its consequences) and much has happened to John Bull since then. It is no longer the duty of a good citizen, as Max courageously felt it to be at that time, to strike the idol of the day in the House of Rimmon, and denounce the excessive adulation of Kipling as leader of the vulgar Jingo chorus.

To judge the totality of an author's work by his politics and by his occasional faults of taste, as Mr. Mortimer seems here for once to do, is not the way to judge a great writer of the past. By such a test we should feel called upon to deprive ourselves of the pleasure of reading *Gulliver*, *The Drapier's Letters* and *The Examiner*, because Swift was a savage and unscrupulous controversialist; because he told extravagant lies about the metallic value of Wood's halfpence; because he wrote a beastly poem, *The Salamander*, accusing Cutts, the bravest man in Marlborough's army, of filthy vices, for no reason but that Swift, being a parson, was jealous of soldiers; while he wrote another poem styling the Duchess of Somerset a murderess, being incensed against her because he thought she advised Queen Anne not to make him a bishop. No, these are not the standards by which we judge the value of Swift's writings. And similar standards of condemnation (*mutatis mutandis*) are equally inapplicable to Kipling, or to any other author whose writings are in question. And in fact there is much less to say against Kipling in such matters than against Swift.

Before I come to Kipling's positive merits, I should like to say something in mitigation of these political and moral failings, which seem to me to have affected overmuch Mr. Mortimer's opinion of his work as a story-teller. The complaint that he did not like the Indian political classes is true, and I regret it. But there were some sides of Indian life, not ignoble ones, into which he had a keen and sympathetic insight, not unworthy of Sir Alfred Lyall in his day and of Jim Corbett in ours. Mr. Mortimer tells us that he himself thinks *Kim* and *The Jungle Book* to be Kipling's best work, but he finds even in them no more than 'an urchin of genius captivating us with day dreams'. I should have thought they contained much penetrating observation. Indeed I wonder that Mr. Mortimer should have read *Kim*, and that other beautiful tale in *The Second Jungle Book* entitled *The Miracle of Purun Bhagat*, of the Prime Minister of an Indian State retiring to end his life as a hermit in the Himalayas, and yet not perceive that Kipling had imaginative sympathy with much that is most peculiarly Indian. Mr. T. S. Eliot has recently written of Kipling: 'In his Indian tales it is on the whole the Indian characters who have the greater reality, because they are treated with *the understanding of love*.' And again—'The first condition of understanding a foreign country is to smell it, as you smell India in *Kim*'. To thrust all this aside, as does Mr. Mortimer, because you disapprove of Kipling's attitude to Indian politicians, is strange; one might as well say that Sir Walter Scott had no sympathy with the Scottish common people, because he took, as I think he did, an ignorant and panicky view of the Radical disturbances in Glasgow in 1819. Scott understood the Scottish burgher and peasant, but not the Scottish factory hand. Kipling understood with intimacy and love many things in Indian life, but not the Congress movement. *Non omnia possumus omnes*. Let us judge a man by his best, not by his worst. In literature above all that surely is the rule. Are we to be prevented from enjoying the fun of *Cashel Byron's Profession*, *Candida*, *Major Barbara* and *Arms and the Man*, because of the immense amount of nonsense on all sorts of subjects that Shaw has elsewhere uttered?

Similarly, are we to forgo the unique pleasure of reading George Borrow's *Lavengro*, because his judgment of men and things, though occasionally shrewd, is often a heap of self-contradictory prejudices, violently expressed, and because he is always talking as if he were a great philologist, whereas he was only a great linguist? But how superb are his gifts of observation and description, and of giving life and power to dialogue! The fact is that genius does not always wear the white robe of blameless common sense and fair minded judgment, without which we little people cannot decently appear in public. Some men of genius have had all-round judgment and common sense, but by no means all of them. We must take them as they are, grumble, and be thankful to have them all the same.

As to brutality and descriptions of cruelty that smudge a few of Kipling's stories, I admit their existence here and there. but they seem to me occasional only, quite outweighed by the vigour and vitality of his story-telling in general, and of less account in our proper conception of the man than the frequent beauty and sympathy of his imagination particularly in *Puck of Pook's Hill*, to which I shall presently return.

Indeed, as regards descriptions of cruelty, I am surprised at Mr. Mortimer's complaint, for there are plenty such in more recent writers which pass muster as up-to-date realism; to complain of them would argue one an old Victorian fogy. But Kipling apparently is protected by no such licence.

I knew Kipling a little towards the end of his life. What struck me about him was his modesty, a quality not universal among the most prominent literary figures after the First World War. This modesty took in particular the form of unquenchable interest in the special work and trained capacity of the person to whom he was talking, whether engineer, craftsman, agricultural labourer, or professional man. He was pleased, when I told him that his stories in *Puck of Pook's Hill* and *Rewards and Fairies* showed a marvellous historical flair. Because I was an historian he valued the compliment and beamed at me. He was what is (I believe) now called "an extrovert", that is to say he was not entirely wrapped up in himself.

This constant interest in other people's jobs was of great value to him, because, as Sir Desmond MacCarthy said, one of the reasons of his just popularity is that his stories tell of people's daily work, not merely of their personal relations. Take for instance his tale called *William the Conqueror*. The interest is not in the heroine's love affair, which is very like any other, at any rate as such things happen in books. The interest and novelty to the reader lie in the realities of an Indian famine and the way it is dealt with by individual members of the I.C.S. Among the stories of English work in India the one I like best of all is *The Tomb of his Ancestors*. It concerns a man's hereditary influence over a primitive hill tribe. The story is concerned only with the life of these attractive little folk and an Englishman's work among them, not at all with his love affairs—such a relief sometimes! And far the best of Kipling's poems is about the relations of a Scottish engineer to his engines.

Among great writers Kipling is not perhaps highly distinguished as a creator of characters that live for ever in the heart and memory of mankind, like Uncle Toby, Dandie Dinmont, Mr. Micawber and Alan Breck Stewart—yet there are Mulvaney, Ortheris and Learoyd. But he is a very great story teller. He is occasionally offensive, often overstrained, but never dull. And besides the excitement and realism of his tales, there is often a hint of the uncanny spiritual powers, working below. He is not a mere realist. *The Finest Story in the World* and *The End of the Passage* are realistic but they are something else besides.

Genius is not so common a thing that we can afford to reject it because of its alloy. I enjoy his stories, and I object to being told that it is bad form for a grown-up to be found reading them, that we "never mention him", that "his name is never heard". It will be heard for a very long time to come.

Perhaps it is because I also have never "grown up"— (should one wholly and in all respects "grow up" I wonder?)— but in any case I confess that the work of Kipling's that I like best of all is *Puck of Pook's Hill* and *Rewards and Fairies*. His return from the East at an early age was I think a most fortunate event. In the hot-house of India his genius had been forced to a premature, exotic blossoming, and he was already the most popular author of his day. But he was still young enough to strike fresh roots. In the open air of the English countryside he found a new subject and purer imagination. When he fell under the charm of rural Sussex, its folk like old Hobden and their traditions, he had a sudden vision of the whole length of our island history. *Puck of Pook's Hill* is natural, beautiful, gentle—if you like, childlike. In a setting of fairyland and childhood the very opposite of brutal, he tells us tale after tale of the ancient history of England, as he imagines it, with a marvellous historical sense I think. The language and the psychology of Romans, Saxons and Normans is frankly modern —"subalterns again" if you like—but as no one knows how the people of those far-gone ages thought or spoke, there is no good using "tushery", and Kipling's way of making them talk is as good as another. But we know a good deal about the historic social surroundings in which they moved, and these Kipling has carefully studied and reproduced. Above all the tales are alive and they are beautiful. The story about Drake, called *Simple Simon* and the story about Harold called *The Tree of Justice* in *Rewards and Fairies* are very striking. As a piece of historical imagination I know nothing in the world better than the third story in *Puck*, called *The Joyous Venture*, in which the Viking ship coasts Africa to find gold and fight gorillas in the tropical forest. I can see no fault in it, and many a merit. The poem attached to it, called *Harp Song of the Dane Women*, has the rare quality of sympathetic historical imagination. Kipling has so entered into the situation and the sorrows of the wives of the Vikings, when their husbands go off for their summer piratings across the Northern Ocean—"the old grey Widow-maker". If you come to think of it, it must have been so. That is how the Viking raids, on their human and domestic side, must have been launched each year. But only Kipling has thought of it without prompting. I will read you the poem:

What is a woman that you forsake her,
And the hearth-fire and the home-acre,
To go with the old grey Widow-maker?

She has no house to lay a guest in—
But one chill bed for all to rest in,
That the pale suns and the stray bergs nest in.

She has no strong white arms to fold you,
But the ten-times-fingering weed to hold you
Bound on the rocks where the tide has rolled you.

Yet, when the signs of summer thicken,
And the ice breaks, and the birch-buds quicken,
Yearly you turn from our side, and sicken—

Sicken again for the shouts and the slaughters,—
You steal away to the lapping waters,
And look at your ship in her winter quarters.

You forget our mirth, and talk at the tables,
The kine in the shed and the horse in the stables—
To pitch her sides and go over her cables!

Then you drive out where the storm-clouds swallow:
And the sound of your oar-blades falling hollow,
Is all we have left through the months to follow.

Ah, what is Woman that you forsake her,
And the hearth-fire and the home-acre,
To go with the old grey Widow-maker?

That may not be great poetry, but it is fine literature, sound and sympathetic history, certainly not the work of a brute or of an "urchin" who never grew up.

Robert Browning is a mid-Victorian poet who, I am told, is little read today, even less I suspect than Kipling, though he is less abused. In appraisement of him I see eye to eye with Mr. Mortimer, as indeed I usually do. Browning has given me so much pleasure, of a higher kind than Kipling, that I cannot but hope that some of you may enjoy him too. In that hope I will tell you a little of my own experience.

One difficulty about learning to love our poets, is that unless you can give a great deal of time to studying them, it is not easy to find their best work, as it is often surrounded by much inferior stuff. There are dreary lengths of Wordsworth, Byron, Shelley, Coleridge, Tennyson. Anthologies may help, but the problem cannot be entirely solved. One or two rough rules for beginners may be useful—such as, keep clear of Shelley's *Queen Mab* and *Revolt of Islam*; start with what Wordsworth wrote before 1810, ere you venture to search the second half of his life's work for scattered fragments of excellence, and above all read *The Prelude* before you try *The Excursion*. Now as regards Browning, my advice to you is to read first and foremost the shorter poems of his middle period, grouped under the headings *Dramatic Romances*, *Men and Women*, *Dramatis Personae*. In the two-volumed edition of his Collected Works (Smith Elder) volume I contains almost all his best.

His life's history as a poet is curious. Instead of beginning with the simple and imitative, and going on to become singular and obscure, he started as a very young man in the eighteen-thirties with very original, very long, but very difficult poems—*Pauline*, *Paracelsus*, *Sordello*. (It was said of *Sordello* that there was only one line in it that could be understood, the first

Who will, may hear Sordello's story told

and that it was not true.) Then he proceeded, in the eighteen-forties, 'fifties and early 'sixties, to write almost all his greatest

work, poems of short or moderate length and sufficient lucidity,
published under the headings I have named to you. Then in the
late eighteen-sixties, when he was fifty-five years old, he wrote
the *Ring and the Book*, a remarkable *tour de force*, but not a good
starting point, until you are very sure you not only like
Browning but want a very great deal of him. After the *Ring and
the Book* he spent his old age in writing shorter poems, rather
in the style but no longer with the power and beauty of the
poems that he had written in his prime. If you read nothing
that he wrote *after* the *Ring and the Book* you will miss very
little. *Dramatic Lyrics*, *Asolando*, *Pacchiarotto*, *Red Cotton Nightcap
Country* and the rest correspond to Wordsworth's later poetry.
With a few exceptions, they are but a shadow of his real work,
the manner without the inspiration.

And so I return to the essential Browning, the Browning
of the eighteen-forties and 'fifties, the Browning of *Dramatic
Romances*, *Men and Women* and *Dramatis Personae*. I will not
speak of the plays of the same period, which though they contain much that is good, cannot escape the general doom of
Nineteenth-century poetic drama, which though written by
our greatest poets did not quite suit either the study or the
stage. *Atalanta in Calydon* is perhaps an exception, where the
form of Greek drama contained Swinburne's exuberance
within limits, while giving him scope for the chorus:

> When the hounds of spring are on winter's traces.

Sometimes, even in Browning's best work, though not
always, he drags in fantastic religious or philosophical ideas
into poems that might be better without them—like the famous
Grammarian's Funeral. But there is nothing of the sort in the
other great poem on the Italian renaissance, *The Bishop orders
his Tomb in St. Praxed's*. And sometimes, perhaps, his philosophic ideas succeed, as in *Abt Vogler*; at least my friend
Vaughan Williams told me more than fifty years ago that
Abt Vogler was just right:

> The rest may reason and welcome: 'tis we musicians know.

But whatever we may think of his philosophy, it is certain that his intellectual power and play and his humour often add to the charm of his work even if sometimes they clash with its beauty. The restless activity of his mind is both the strength and the weakness of his poetry. Here are three poems to illustrate his peculiar merits—there are a hundred others that would do as well. First '*De Gustibus*.'

I

Your ghost will walk, you lover of trees,
    (If our loves remain)
    In an English lane,
By a cornfield-side a-flutter with poppies.
Hark, those two in the hazel coppice—
A boy and a girl, if the good fates please,
    Making love, say,—
    The happier they!
Draw yourself up from the light of the moon,
And let them pass, as they will too soon,
    With the bean-flowers' boon,
    And the blackbird's tune,
    And May, and June!

II

What I love best in all the world
Is a castle, precipice-encurled,
In a gash of the wind-grieved Apennine.
Or look for me, old fellow of mine,
(If I get my head from out the mouth
O' the grave, and loose my spirit's bands,
And come again to the land of lands)—
In a sea-side house to the farther South,
Where the baked cicala dies of drouth,
And one sharp tree—'tis a cypress—stands,
By the many hundred years red-rusted,
Rough iron-spiked, ripe fruit-o'ercrusted,
My sentinel to guard the sands
To the water's edge. For, what expands

Before the house, but the great opaque
Blue breadth of sea without a break?
While, in the house, for ever crumbles
Some fragment of the frescoed walls,
From blisters where a scorpion sprawls.
A girl bare-footed brings, and tumbles
Down on the pavement, green-flesh melons,
And says there's news to-day—the king
Was shot at, touched in the liver-wing,
Goes with his Bourbon arm in a sling:
—She hopes they have not caught the felons.
Italy, my Italy!
Queen Mary's saying serves for me—
    (When fortune's malice
    Lost her—Calais)—
Open my heart and you will see
Graved inside of it, "Italy".
Such lovers old are I and she:
So it always was, so shall ever be!

Then take the little double poem, describing a lover beaching his boat and going up to his *rendez-vous* at night, and coming away again in the morning.

Meeting at Night

The grey sea and the long black land;
And the yellow half-moon large and low;
And the startled little waves that leap
In fiery ringlets from their sleep,
As I gain the cove with pushing prow,
And quench its speed i' the slushy sand.
Then a mile of warm sea-scented beach;
Three fields to cross till a farm appears;
A tap at the pane, the quick sharp scratch
And blue spurt of a lighted match,
And a voice less loud, thro' its joys and fears,
Than the two hearts beating each to each!

Parting at Morning

Round the cape of a sudden came the sea,
And the sun looked over the mountain's rim:

And straight was a path of gold for him,
And the need of a world of men for me.

Browning rightly called himself a dramatic poet, not in the
sense that he succeeded in writing for the stage, but in the sense
that most of his poems are written to explain or to impersonate
people not himself. In this he was the opposite of Wordsworth,
who when he tried in *The Excursion* to make several other
people speak, only repeated himself clumsily, whereas when he
spoke for and of himself alone in *The Prelude*, he succeeded
admirably. Take Browning's poem *Up at a Villa—Down in the
City*, where he impersonates an impoverished Italian nobleman, yet manages very skilfully to infiltrate into the silly old
gentleman's grumblings a good deal of his own poetry and
humour.

Up at a Villa—Down in the City

(As distinguished by an Italian person of quality.)

Had I but plenty of money, money enough and to spare,
The house for me, no doubt, were a house in the city-square;
Ah, such a life, such a life, as one leads at the window there!
Something to see, by Bacchus, something to hear, at least!
There, the whole day long, one's life is a perfect feast;
While up at a villa one lives, I maintain it, no more than a beast.

Well now, look at our villa! stuck like the horn of a bull
Just on a mountain-edge as bare as the creature's skull,
Save a mere shag of a bush with hardly a leaf to pull!
—I scratch my own, sometimes, to see if the hair's turned wool.

But the city, oh the city—the square with the houses! Why?
They are stone-faced, white as a curd, there's something to take
    the eye!
Houses in four straight lines, not a single front awry;
You watch who crosses and gossips, who saunters, who hurries
    by;
Green blinds, as a matter of course, to draw when the sun gets
    high;
And the shops with fanciful signs which are painted properly.

What of a villa? Though winter be over in March by rights,
'Tis May perhaps ere the snow shall have withered well off the
heights:
You've the brown ploughed land before, where the oxen steam
and wheeze,
And the hills over-smoked behind by the faint grey olive-trees.

Is it better in May, I ask you? You've summer all at once;
In a day he leaps complete with a few strong April suns.
'Mid the sharp short emerald wheat, scarce risen three fingers well,
The wild tulip at end of its tube, blows out its great red bell
Like a thin clear bubble of blood, for the children to pick and sell.

Is it ever hot in the square? There's a fountain to spout and
splash!
In the shade it sings and springs; in the shine such foam-bows
flash
On the horses with curling fish-tails, that prance and paddle and
pash
Round the lady atop in her conch—fifty gazers do not abash,
Though all that she wears is some weeds round her waist in a sort
of sash.

All the year long at the villa, nothing to see though you linger,
Except yon cypress that points like death's lean lifted forefinger.
Some think fireflies pretty, when they mix i' the corn and mingle,
Or thrid the stinking hemp till the stalks of it seem a-tingle.
Late August or early September, the stunning cicala is shrill,
And the bees keep their tiresome whine round the resinous firs on
the hill.
Enough of the seasons—I spare you the months of the fever and
chill.

Ere you open your eyes in the city, the blessed church-bells begin:
No sooner the bells leave off than the diligence rattles in:
You get the pick of the news, and it costs you never a pin.
By-and-by there's the travelling doctor gives pills, lets blood,
draws teeth;
Or the Pulcinello-trumpet breaks up the market beneath.
At the post-office such a scene-picture—the new play, piping hot!
And a notice how, only this morning, three liberal thieves were
shot.

Above it, behold the Archbishop's most fatherly of rebukes,
And beneath, with his crown and his lion, some little new law of
  the Duke's!
Or a sonnet with flowery marge, to the Reverend Don So-and-so
Who is Dante, Boccaccio, Petrarca, Saint Jerome and Cicero,
"And moreover" (the sonnet goes rhyming) "the skirts of Saint
  Paul has reached,
"Having preached us those six Lent-lectures more unctuous than
  ever he preached."
Noon strikes,—here sweeps the procession! our Lady borne smiling
  and smart
With a pink gauze gown all spangles, and seven swords stuck in
  her heart!
Bang-whang-whang goes the drum, *tootle-te-tootle* the fife;
No keeping one's haunches still: it's the greatest pleasure in life.

But bless you, it's dear—it's dear! fowls, wine, at double the rate.
They have clapped a new tax upon salt, and what oil pays passing
  the gate
It's a horror to think of. And so, the villa for me, not the city!
Beggars can scarcely be choosers: but still—ah, the pity, the
  pity!
Look, two and two go the priests, then the monks with cowls and
  sandals,
And the penitents dressed in white shirts, a-holding the yellow
  candles;
One, he carries a flag up straight, and another a cross with
  handles
And the Duke's guard brings up the rear, for the better prevention
  of scandals:
Bang-whang-whang goes the drum, *tootle-te-tootle* the fife.
Oh, a day in the city-square, there is no such pleasure in life.

People sometimes say they can't stand Browning because he
was such an optimist. Well, he lived in the Nineteenth not in
the Twentieth Century. His experience was more encouraging
than ours. But what have optimism or pessimism got to do
with the poems I have just read? Moreover it is easy to
exaggerate Browning's optimism. Mr. Raymond Mortimer, in

the excellent article on Browning which opens the fine series of his *Channel Packet* essays, very truly says:

> I think that Browning not only surpassed his English contemporaries in his awareness of evil, but came nearer to ourselves in his sense of what evil is. A passionate absorption in life, comparable to that of Balzac, whom he greatly admired, swept him away from the primness of a Tennyson or an Arnold—look, for instance, at *Respectability*, *Confessions*, *A Light Woman*, *Two in the Campagna*, *The Statue and the Bust*. His optimism is that of the adventurer, not of the muffish recluse who averts his eyes from unpleasant facts.

That, I think, is well said. It is no roseate picture of mankind that Browning paints for us. Objection is sometimes taken to him, on the ground of his optimism, because in the very tragic drama, called *Pippa Passes*, brim full of murders and treacheries, he makes by way of contrast an innocent Italian factory girl sing a number of charming songs, one of which runs thus:

> The year's at the spring
> And day's at the morn;
> Morning's at seven;
> The hill-side's dew-pearled;
> The lark's on the wing;
> The snail's on the thorn:
> God's in his heaven—
> All's right with the world!

Why on earth should anybody object to the last two lines taken in their context?

In the book entitled *Siegfried's Journey 1916–1920*, valuable above all for the very beautiful pictures it gives of Thomas Hardy in his old age, Sassoon tells us that he once asked him "why *Ah, did you once see Shelley plain?* is such a memorable poem". Hardy replied "Because Browning wrote from his heart".

> Ah, did you once see Shelley plain,
> And did he stop and speak to you
> And did you speak to him again?
> How strange it seems and new!

But you were living before that,
  And also you are living after;
And the memory I started at—
  My starting moves your laughter.

I crossed a moor, with a name of its own
  And a certain use in the world no doubt,
Yet a hand's-breadth of it shines alone
  'Mid the blank miles round about:

For there I picked up on the heather
  And there I put inside my breast
A moulted feather, an eagle-feather!
  Well, I forget the rest.

III

I SPOKE, at the end of my last lecture, of Robert Browning. If you seek his exact opposite, both as a man and as a writer, consider one of the long line of poets of whom Trinity can boast—A. E. Housman. Browning loved life; Housman endured it. Browning loved men; Housman pitied them. Browning wrote many kinds of verse—narrative, drama, lyric, in many different moods; Housman had one method and one mood, though he commanded a variety of metres. Browning was the greater poet and the greater man; Housman the more invariably perfect artist. Browning was a flooded river, fed from mountain sources, rioting over the plain and often overflowing the banks; Housman was a quiet stream threading its way through frozen meadows. Browning gave his whole life to the composition of poetry; Housman spent most of his time on scholarship, and only occasionally was attacked in his vitals by an urge to write down a few verses. Browning wrote of men and women of all sorts, conditions and dates in time; Housman wrote of himself, and when he spoke of other men gave no picture of them as individuals, but only as victims of fate. Browning was by temperament optimistic; speaking for once in his own person, he tells us he

> Never doubted clouds would break,
> Never dreamed, though right were worsted,
> > wrong would triumph.

Housman was a Stoic

> Therefore, since the world has still
> Much good, but much less good than ill,
> And while the sun and moon endure
> Luck's a chance, but trouble's sure,
> I'd face it as a wise man should
> And train for ill and not for good.

44

Housman I say was a Stoic. He may have been a pessimist,
but he certainly was not a cynic. He was as much on the side
of the angels as Browning, but he thought that it was a losing
battle. He loved virtue and friendship. He was keenly alive to
the beauty of nature, and to the glory of men in their youth.
But he saw everything under shadow of doom. He is always
telling us that "trouble" is the common lot.

> The troubles of our proud and angry dust
> Are from eternity and shall not fail.

You may say that his most constant theme is an enlargement
on three lines of Chaucer.

> What is this world? What axen men to have?
> Now with his love, now in his colde grave
> Alone withouten any compagnie.

In the *Shropshire Lad*, written in the early eighteen-nineties, he
was obsessed overmuch by the idea of the death of the young,
and seemed to make it happen oftener than the average of
facts then warranted. But we soon found more wholesale
methods of killing the young, so that the war of 1914–18, that
altered the outlook of so many of us, gave him no reason to
change his philosophy. In *Last Poems* he treats that world
catastrophe very quietly, almost casually, as part of the known
nature of things:

> 'Tis true there's better boose than brine,
>   but he that drowns must drink it.

> The Spartans on the sea-wet rock sat
>   down and combed their hair.

"Fellows that were good and brave" "died because they
were"—Naturally!

To my thinking his most perfect, and in spite of its brevity
his greatest, poem is *On Wenlock Edge*. (The MS. was placed on
exhibition in the Library of his College during his lifetime, a
rare honour.) It seems to me to combine beauty, of words and
of feeling, and pregnant thought with a pattern of intellectual

construction unusual even in great poetry. I will read it through first and then analyse it a little. The scene is laid in Shropshire, at Wroxeter, by the ruins of the Roman city of Uricon, looking up at the steep wooded height of the Wrekin, beyond which flows the Severn.

> On Wenlock Edge the wood's in trouble;
> His forest fleece the Wrekin heaves;
> The gale, it plies the saplings double,
> And thick on Severn snow the leaves.
>
> 'Twould blow like this through holt and hanger
> When Uricon the city stood:
> 'Tis the old wind in the old anger,
> But then it threshed another wood.
>
> Then, 'twas before my time, the Roman
> At yonder heaving hill would stare:
> The blood that warms an English yeoman,
> The thoughts that hurt him, they were there.
>
> There, like the wind through woods in riot,
> Through him the gale of life blew high;
> The tree of man was never quiet:
> Then 'twas the Roman, now 'tis I.
>
> The gale, it plies the saplings double,
> It blows so hard, 'twill soon be gone:
> To-day the Roman and his trouble
> Are ashes under Uricon.

Surely it has, as I say, a perfectly constructed pattern of intellectual composition that adds greatly to the poetic feeling. The simile sustained throughout is the wind blowing through the trees, as trouble blows through the heart of man. There is still the same wind, and still same doom of trouble, as in Roman times "when Uricon the city stood". Only now, since the woods decay and fall, "another wood" clothes the Wrekin in place of the old, and an Englishman stands with the ashes of the Roman under his feet. But the wind still blows through the new wood, and trouble ("the gale of life") through the

heart of the modern man. Trees and men are shortlived; the
wind and the trouble that vex them are eternal.

Such is the pattern of the thought. And I cannot conceive
that any poet could have elaborated a more perfectly artistic
and beautiful way of working out the pattern in the successive
verses. The marriage of intellect with feeling is consummate.

But how could poems in this one constant mood of grim
stoicism ever have been as popular as they were? Well, in the
first place they are not one long poem but a series of short
pieces, with great variation of metre and each presenting a
new scene, thought or person. But the chief thing that catches
and holds the reader is the amazing skill and beauty of the
verse, often containing most pregnant phrases.

> To think that two and two are four
> And neither five nor three
> The heart of man has long been sore
> And long 'tis like to be.

Moreover the mortal tragedy is relieved by lines describing
the beauties of nature, a motif which, though he would turn
it also to sadness, is in fact calculated to make us happy. It is
the dominant note in many of the poems, as in

> " Loveliest of trees, the cherry now."
>
> " In valleys of springs of rivers."
>
> " Far in a Western brookland."

> Tell me not here, it needs not saying,
>   What tune the enchantress plays
> In aftermaths of soft September
>   Or under blanching mays,
> For she and I were long acquainted
>   And I knew all her ways.
>
> On russet floors, by waters idle,
>   The pine lets fall its cone;
> The cuckoo shouts all day at nothing
>   In leafy dells alone;
> And traveller's joy beguiles in autumn
>   Hearts that have lost their own.

On acres of the seeded grasses
　　The changing burnish heaves;
Or marshalled under moons of harvest
　　Stand still all night the sheaves;
Or beeches strip in storms for winter
　　And stain the wind with leaves.

Possess, as I possessed a season,
　　The countries I resign,
Where over elmy plains the highway
　　Would mount the hills and shine,
And full of shade the pillared forest
　　Would murmur and be mine.

For nature, heartless, witless nature
　　Will neither care nor know
What stranger's feet may find the meadow
　　And trespass there and go,
Nor ask amid the dews of morning
　　If they are mine or no.

There have been many magical words said about the cuckoo, especially by Wordsworth, but nothing more magical than

　　The cuckoo shouts all day at nothing
　　　　In leafy dells alone.

And again

　　Or marshalled under moons of harvest
　　　　Stand still all night the sheaves—

is so beautiful a thought and picture of the old agricultural world that nurtured our English poets, that one welcomes the combined harvester with a suppressed sigh.

It is indeed a lovely poem. But the last verse, for all its beauty, is an example of the sadness with which Housman insists on tinging everything. He is sad because "heartless, witless nature" "will neither care nor know" when he dies and comes no more to "possess" her gifts. I have not this feeling. The Wordsworthian joy in nature is not dimmed for me by the knowledge that I shall not possess it for ever. We come

and pass and are not, but nature remains, the friend of each
of us in turn. The mountains that look down on me were there
long before me and will be long after—a thought that makes
their friendship dearer and the strength they give me stronger,
for they typify lastingness. I prefer the sentiment of Matthew
Arnold's words, in his poem called *Switzerland*.

> Blow, ye winds! lift me with you!
>   I come to the wild.
> Fold closely, O Nature!
>   Thine arms round thy child.
>
> To thee only God granted
>   A heart ever new—
> To all always open,
>   To all always true.
>
> Ah! calm me, restore me;
>   And dry up my tears
> On thy high mountain-platforms,
>   Where morn first appears;
>
> Where the white mists, for ever,
>   Are spread and upfurl'd—
> In the stir of the forces
>   Whence issued the world.

Yes, Nature is

> To all always open
> To all always true.

How then could she make a particular pet of me?

Mountain scenery is by no means all of nature's gifts to us,
or the most usual or easy of access. But as I have been led by
Arnold's lines to mention mountains, I will go on. You will
find little about them in our earlier literature, because it is
only since the last half of the Eighteenth Century that anything
higher than a green hill gave pleasure to man. The old ballad-
maker put it tersely:

> "And what is that mountain there?" she said,
>   "So dreary with frost and snow?"
> "O that is the mountain of hell," he said,
>   "Where you and I must go."

Even when Milton approves of

> Mountains on whose barren breast
> The labouring clouds do often rest.

they are not very high, or very near; they only come in as a distant background to

> Russet Lawns and Fallows grey,
> Where the nibbling flocks do stray,

and

> Meadows trim with Daisies pied,
> Shallow brooks and rivers wide.

For the rest, there are "frozen Alps" in Milton's Hell, but none in his Paradise or in his Heaven.

But as soon as mountains began to seem delectable objects in themselves, to be studied and loved for their own sakes, Wordsworth made them the basis of a system of poetical philosophy, and Shelley wrote some fine lines on Alpine scenery, and Coleridge his great Chamouni hymn. That generation first put the stamp of poetry on the mountain world, seeking it out as vigorous pedestrians, traversing the Lake Hills, or crossing the lower slopes and passes of the Alps. Blessed was Jones of Johns, who went on the walking tour that was the *prelude* to so much.

But two generations later came a new class of observer, the Alpinist or mountain climber, to whom new scenes were revealed, and by whom new emotions were felt. These experiences of the roped brotherhood in regions to which few of us can penetrate, soon found their place in English literature through Leslie Stephen's *Playground of Europe.*

You are [he writes] in the first place, perched on a cliff, whose presence is the more felt because it is unseen. Then you are in a region over which eternal silence is brooding. Not a sound ever comes there, except the occasional fall of a splintered fragment of rock, or a layer of snow; no stream is heard trickling, and the sounds of animal life are left thousands of feet below. The most that you can hear is some mysterious noise made by the wind eddying round the gigantic rocks; sometimes a strange flapping sound, as if an unearthly flag was shaking its invisible folds in the air. The enormous tract of country over which your view extends—most of it dim and almost dissolved into air by distance —intensifies the strange influence of the silence. You feel the force of the line I have quoted from Wordsworth—

The sleep that is among the lonely hills.

None of the travellers whom you can see crawling at your feet has the least conception of what is meant by the silent solitudes of the High Alps. To you, it is like a return to the stir of active life, when, after hours of lonely wandering, you return to hear the tinkling of the cow-bells below; to them the same sound is the ultimate limit of the habitable world.

Leslie Stephen not only gave literary expression to the experience of the climber of the highest peaks in summer, but he also, in the same book, in the fine essay entitled *The Alps in Winter*, pictures the lower mountain region, snowbound at that season, into which he was one of the first Englishmen to penetrate before the era of ski-ing.

In the winter Alps, he tells us:

the very daylight has an unreal glow. The noisy summer life is suspended. A scarce audible hush seems to be whispered throughout the region. The first glacier stream that you meet strikes the keynote of the prevailing melody. In summer the torrent comes down like a charge of cavalry—all rush and roar and foam and fury—turbid with the dust ground from the mountain's flanks by the ice-share, and spluttering and writhing in its bed like a creature in the agonies of strangulation. In winter it is transformed into the likeness of one of the gentle brooks that creeps round the roots of Scawfell, or even one of those sparkling trout-streams that slide through a water-meadow beneath Stonehenge. It is perfectly transparent. It babbles round rocks instead of clearing them at a bound. It can at most fret away the edges of the huge white pillows of snow that cap the boulders. High up it can only show itself at intervals between smothering snow-beds which form continuous bridges. Even the thundering fall of the Handeck becomes a gentle thread of pure water creeping behind a broad sheet of ice, more delicately carved and moulded than a lady's veil, and so diminished in volume that one wonders how it has managed to festoon the broad rock faces with so vast a mass of pendent icicles. The pulse of the mountains is beating low; the huge arteries through which the life-blood courses so furiously in summer have become a world too wide for this trickle of pellucid water. If one is still forced to attribute personality to the peaks, they are clearly in a state of suspended animation. They are spell-bound, dreaming of dim abysses of past time or of the summer that is to recall them to life. They are in a trance like that of the Ancient Mariner when he heard strange spirit voices conversing overhead in mysterious murmurs.

If Leslie Stephen celebrated the Alps in prose-poetry, there is also a poet of modern mountaineering, my own friend and contemporary Geoffrey Winthrop Young. Of later writers I am incompetent to speak, for as Mr. Mortimer has most truly said (*Channel Packet*, p. 111) 'where poetry is concerned most men remain faithful to their adolescent taste'. Being well aware of this limiting rule, I do not, as you may observe, attempt to speak of poets who have arisen since my "adolescent taste" was formed. I know my frontier.

But Geoffrey Winthrop Young was my contemporary at Trinity and I intend now to speak of him. He has been recognized by his fellow mountaineers as their poet, and I think that we too, though "our low life is the level's", can appreciate what he writes of *High Hills*:

> There is much comfort in high hills,
> and a great easing of the heart.
> We look upon them, and our nature fills
> with loftier images from their life apart.
> They set our feet on curves of freedom, bent
> to snap the circles of our discontent.
>
> Mountains are moods; of larger rhythm and line,
> moving between the eternal mode and mine.

Moments in thought, of which I too am part,
I lose in them my instant of brief ills.—
There is great easing of the heart,
and cumulance of comfort on high hills.

I could quote much that Geoffrey Young has excellently
written of the mountains, but I will only read one other of his
Alpine scenes, on the subject of *A Glacier Pool*. The climbing
party is descending from an attempt, wearied out and defeated,
and are revived by a plunge in the ice cold water: it is the best
account of a bathe that I know in poetry:

Back from the summit; every muscle aching
    from jarring harsh descent;
the will alert, and eye and nerve yet waking;
    spirit and strength half spent.

Back from the summit; victory denied us,
    retreat alone before;
no more the gates of mountain hope to guide us;
    only the hostel door.

By blind white slopes where treacherously lingers
    the melted morning stair;
by hot dry rocks, that scorch the weary fingers
    clenched with insistent care;

choked with the grit and dust of barren ranges,
    parched with the pitiless snow,
heavy with sleepless night and strident changes
    from frost to furnace-glow;

all that is left, monotony of faring
    on sullen stumbling feet
along the interminable glacier, glaring
    with white uneasy heat. . . .

A sudden thrill of change! The ice-plain, riven,
    yawns in a vast cold break,
where from the depths a flash of mirrored heaven
    reveals the glacial lake.

Sheer from our feet luminous cliffs uplifting
  stark pinnacles and capes:
far on the sapphire surface idly drifting
  fantastic crystal shapes;

and ever and again a boom of thunder,
  the swash of unseen falls,
as some ice-promontory rent asunder
  breaks from the caverned walls.

Rest for our eyes, in this translucent seeing;
  breath, in its silent cool;
and all earth's promise of recovered being
  deep from the sun-starred pool. . . .

Lo, with the thought, we stoop in still desire,
  poised o'er the azure face:
then, in one flame-lash of engulfing fire,
  plunge through the iced embrace:—

Shrill rush of night, where the blanched cliffs descending
  shimmer green-lit and dim;
a stabbing ecstasy of ice-chill rending
  sloth from each jaded limb;

no breath, nor thought, save of the snow-froth hissing
  round fever-laden frame;
chill on the lips the waves' delicious kissing,
  vein-drafts of frozen flame;

cold throbs of life, bright as the bubbles surging
  from the swift-circling hand;
speed as of gods, in every movement urging
  the flakes chattering to land;

on throat and hair the brittle ice-stars breaking
  like foam of silver wine;
floods of exultant sense, starkly awaking
  a vigour of youth divine. . . .

Toil to delight, pain to remembered pleasure,
  embers to ruddy gold
change at thy touch, O life's most usual treasure,
  water, divinely cold!

There is an edition of Geoffrey Young's *Collected Poems*, Methuen, 1936.

I return to scenes more familiar to most of us. Though Wordsworth, both as poet and philosopher, makes such magnificent use of the peasantry of the Lake District, he never attempts their dialect; his Michael talks in south English blank verse. Indeed the poet remains in some respects aloof from the farming population whom he praises, regarding them sympathetically from outside. For the peasantry of that region seen from the inside, as they really think and talk, I commend you to the poems of Miss Margaret Cropper, particularly her two beautiful and most human narrative poems *Little Mary Crosbie* and *The End of the Road*. I do not think they have received the general attention that they deserve. And her shorter poems, such as *The Broken Hearth Stone*, are the most faithful poetic rendering of that region in its detail. Her merit as a poetess is that her deepest feeling is wedded to acutest observation. I cannot I fear illustrate to you her strongest side, her reproduction of the life, character and dialect of the inhabitants of the Lake valleys, as it would require such long quotations. But here is a short poem, that could only have been written on a hill farm. It is called *The Grey Ewe*:

> The sheep, that are so silent all the winter,
> Have in this mothering time found their voices
> To admonish their sweet, daredevil children,
> And to comfort them in a hundred transient distresses.
> The ewe's voice . . . almost you might think
> The grey rock had taken to itself speech;
> So harshly tender it is, so roughly consoling;
> The ewe's voice, that has the Winter in it,
> The old endurance of Nature's pain.
> The grey ewe . . . aye, maybe she is the Winter,
> And this leaping, trustful little venturer
> Is the wild Spring that has come from her dark womb.

If any of you wish to study Miss Cropper's poems further, they have been many of them collected in the volume entitled

The End of the Road (Thomas Nelson, 1935), which contains also *Little Mary Crosbie*. If you fail to get it supplied by your own bookseller, write to Mr. Roberts, Mickle Street, Kendal.

Poets often insert geographic or topographical names in their verses with good effect. I want to illustrate and discuss their practice in this matter a little. I will begin, very quietly, with the first verse of Mickle's *Ballad of Cumnor Hall*, which so enchanted the youthful Walter Scott that he never forgot the story and long afterwards wrote *Kenilworth*.

> The dews of summer night did fall;
>   The moon, sweet regent of the sky,
> Silver'd the walls of Cumnor Hall
>   And many an oak that grew thereby.

Mickle was not a great poet, but that is a good verse, and presents a pleasant picture. My point is that it gains, as poetry, by the insertion of the name—Cumnor. Why? First, because Cumnor is a beautiful word. Secondly, because the particularizing of the moonlight scene in a definite place makes us believe more in its reality. And lastly, if we happen to know beforehand about the tragedy of Amy Robsart it suggests much besides the moon and the oaks.

Compare this to another picture, also of a calm midnight in woodland scenery, but of a very different order of poetry— from *Hyperion*.

> As when, upon a tranced summer-night
> Those green-robed senators of mighty woods,
> Tall oaks, branch-charmed by the earnest stars,
> Dream, and so dream all night without a stir,
> Save from one gradual solitary gust
> Which comes upon the silence, and dies off,
> As if the ebbing air had but one wave;
>   So came these words and went.

Here, you will observe, Keats intrudes no topographical name. The beauty of the lines needs no such strengthening; indeed they would be weakened by any such distraction. We are among the gods and Titans, and our thoughts are universal.

The oaks may be either in England or in Arcady, we are too
absorbed in their midnight beauty to ask or care.

Yet geographic names are often brought into the very
greatest poems, even those dealing with universal themes,
when the theme is in danger of getting monotonously universal
and vague, and requires the relief of something terrestrial and
definite. *Paradise Lost* is full of this device, which shocked the
unpoetic pedantry of the greatest of the Masters of Trinity.

Satan's flight from Hell to Earth is illustrated by two such
geographic passages:

> As when far off at sea a fleet descried
> Hangs in the clouds, by equinoctial winds
> Close sailing from Bengala, or the isles
> Of Ternate and Tidore, whence merchants bring
> Their spicy drugs: they on the trading flood
> Through the wide Aethiopian to the Cape
> Ply, stemming nightly toward the pole: so seem'd
> Far off the flying fiend.

And later when he gets near enough to Paradise to scent its
delicious odours:

> As when to them who sail
> Beyond the Cape of Hope, and now are past
> Mozambic, off at sea north-east winds blow
> Sabean odours from the spicy shore
> Of Araby the blest, with such delay
> Well pleased they slack their course, and many a league
> Cheer'd with the grateful smell old Ocean smiles.
> So entertain'd those odorous sweets the fiend
> Who came their bane.

In another passage we even get a glimpse of Galileo, "the
Tuscan artist", viewing the moon through his "optic glass"

> from the top of Fesole
> Or in Valdarno,

and on the very next page the prostrate fiends lie on the floor
of Hell

> Thick as autumnal leaves that strow the brooks
> In Vallombrosa, where th' Etruscan shades
> High overarched embower.

Those rich Italian place-names, Valdarno, Fesole, Vallom-
brosa, rich in sound, rich in historical suggestion, are worthy
to relieve the sometimes oppressive immensity of *Paradise Lost*.
Again the long history of the wars of mankind are reviewed in
a series of high-sounding geographic names. Satan marshals
his embattled hosts:

> And now his heart
> Distends with pride, and hard'ning in his strength
> Glories; for never, since created man,
> Met such embodied force, as named with these
> Could merit more than that small infantry
> Warr'd on by cranes; though all the giant brood
> Of Phlegra with th' heroic race were join'd
> That fought at Thebes and Ilium, on each side
> Mix'd with auxiliar Gods; and what resounds
> In fable or romance of Uther's son,
> Begirt with British and Armoric knights;
> And all who since, baptized or infidel,
> Jousted in Aspramont or Montalban,
> Damasco, or Marocco, or Trebisond,
> Or whom Biserta sent from Afric shore,
> When Charlemain with all his peerage fell
> By Fontarabia.

There is another great poem that owes much to the use of
place names. Indeed I wonder whether the beauty of the
regional names was not one of the attractions that drew
Matthew Arnold to write *Sohrab and Rustum*. At any rate he
makes loving use of such names as Ader-Baijan, Seistan, Kai
Kosroo and Afrasiab's cities, 'Samarcand, Bohkara and lone
Khiva in the waste'. And the poem ends on what is perhaps
the finest piece of geographic poetry in our language:

> But the majestic river floated on,
> Out of the mist and hum of that low land,
> Into the frosty starlight, and there moved,
> Rejoicing, through the hush'd Chorasmian waste,
> Under the solitary moon; he flow'd
> Right for the polar star, past Orgunjè,
> Brimming, and bright, and large; then sands begin

To hem his watery march, and dam his streams,
And split his currents; that for many a league
The shorn and parcell'd Oxus strains along
Through beds of sand and matted rushy isles—
Oxus, forgetting the bright speed he had
In his high mountain-cradle in Pamere,
A foil'd circuitous wanderer—till at last
The long'd-for dash of waves is heard, and wide
His luminous home of waters opens, bright
And tranquil, from whose floor the new-bathed stars
Emerge, and shine upon the Aral Sea.

And in *Thyrsis* he makes fine play with the beautiful names of the higher Thames Valley.

Wordsworth occasionally uses an unexpected place name with magical effect. I am not talking about the group of poems called *Poems on the naming of places*, which are not his best work. But take the short poem with the very long title:

> To a Young Lady
> Who had been reproached for taking
> long walks in the country

It begins:

> "Dear Child of Nature, let them rail",

and then promises her the blessings that accrue to the good walker throughout life. The last of the three stanzas runs thus:

> Thy thoughts and feelings shall not die,
> Nor leave thee, when grey hairs are nigh,
> A melancholy slave;
> But an old age serene and bright
> And lovely as a Lapland night
> Shall lead thee to thy grave.

The word *Lapland* is utterly unexpected, and I maintain, magical in mysterious suggestion. And again in *The Solitary Reaper*, the song of the girl reaping in the Highland strath is set off by two geographic comparisons:

> No nightingale did ever chaunt
> More welcome notes to weary bands

5

Of travellers in some shady haunt
Among Arabian sands:
A voice so thrilling ne'er was heard
In spring time from the cuckoo bird,
Breaking the silence of the seas
Among the farthest Hebrides.

The beauty of the word "Arabian" was never put to better use. And the last two lines about the cuckoo come as a surprise, fraught with a strange magic. The cuckoo, for whom we usually listen "in leafy dells" or inland valleys, is here heard across the silent spaces of ocean "among the farthest Hebrides".

Let us turn for a moment from poetry to prose, for the use of a list of geographic names to produce a literary effect. Here is a bit of prose that bids fair to outlast even the stirring couplets of Addison as a memorial of the *Campaign* that ended at Blenheim. In *Tristram Shandy* those two dear people Corporal Trim and Uncle Toby are talking together as usual:

> What business, added the Corporal triumphantly, has a soldier, an' please your Honour, to know anything at all of *geography*? . . . Thou wouldst have said *chronology*, Trim, said my Uncle Toby; for as for geography, 'tis of absolute use to him. . . . Is it else to be conceived, Corporal, continued my Uncle Toby, rising up in his sentry-box as he began to warm in this part of his discourse— how Marlborough could have marched his army from the banks of the Maes to Belburg; from Belburg to Kerpenord—(here the Corporal could sit no longer)—from Kerpenord, Trim, to Kalsaken; from Kalsaken to Newdorf; from Newdorf to Louden-bourg; from Loudenbourg to Mildenheim; from Mildenheim to Elchingen; from Elchingen to Gingen; from Gingen to Balmer-choffen; from Balmerchoffen to Skellenbourg, where he broke in upon the enemy's works, forced his passage over the Danube, crossed the Lech—pushed on his troops into the heart of the Empire, marching at the head of them through Friburg, Hocken-wert and Schonevelt, to the plains of Blenheim and Hochstet. Great as he was, Corporal, he could not have advanced a step, or made a single day's march without the aids of geography.

Well, "the aids of geography" are sometimes of service to poets also.

The poet who gained most by "the aids of geography" was Macaulay. This was only natural, for he was a writer of historical ballads, not aiming at the higher altitudes of poetry. But what he aimed at he hit.

The *Armada* is perhaps the most geographic poem in our language. It has for ever associated our thought of the Armada with the beacons speeding their message of alarm across the island from hill to hill and shire to shire. Because of Macaulay's ballad, which in those days "every schoolboy knew", the Queen's first Jubilee of 1887, as I well remember, was celebrated by preparing and lighting "the Armada beacons". By hitting on that happy thought of the beacons, Macaulay takes us on a rapid tour of Elizabethan England, with its 'shepherds of Stonehenge and rangers of Beaulieu' and the rest, till he wisely breaks off when 'the red glare of Skiddaw' has 'roused the burghers of Carlisle.' He calls it "a fragment," but it is complete within its limit, when the night alarm has sped from Plymouth to Carlisle, from the tower of 'Ely's stately fane' to 'the stormy hills of Wales', and all England has been roused ere dawn.

Tennyson's ballad of Elizabethan warfare—*The Revenge*—seems to have started in his mind from the sound of place names. Tennyson wrote at the head of a sheet of paper (now in Trinity College Library) the words:

> At Flores in the Azores Sir Richard Grenville lay

and left that first line without sequel, till years later he took it up again and wrote the splendid thing we know.

But to return to the uses of geography in Macaulay's ballads. In *Horatius* the gathering of the Tuscans to follow Lars Porsena to Rome is thus described:

> The horsemen and the footmen
>   Are pouring in amain
> From many a stately market-place;
>   From many a fruitful plain;
> From many a lonely hamlet,
>   Which, hid by beech and pine,

> Like an eagle's nest, hangs on the crest
>   Of purple Apennine;
>
> From lordly Volaterrae,
>   Where scowls the far-famed hold
> Piled by the hands of giants
>   For godlike kings of old;
> From seagirt Populonia,
>   Whose sentinels descry
> Sardinia's snowy mountain-tops
>   Fringing the southern sky;
>
> From the proud mart of Pisae,
>   Queen of the western waves,
> Where ride Massilia's triremes
>   Heavy with fair-haired slaves;
> From where sweet Clanis wanders
>   Through corn and vines and flowers;
> From where Cortona lifts to heaven
>   Her diadem of towers.

Now those of you who have travelled in Italy and approached these places, either driving or, as I have done, on foot will be aware that the visible and historical identity of each is powerfully and beautifully rendered in a very few words. Macaulay, I think, saw that he was making a success of this geographic business, for in the next Lay, of *Lake Regillus*, he gave a similar roll call of the Latin hosts encamped against the Roman, including the lines:

> From where the Witch's Fortress
>   O'erhangs the dark-blue seas;
> From the still glassy lake that sleeps
>   Beneath Aricia's trees—
> Those trees in whose dim shadow
>   The ghastly priest doth reign,
> The priest who slew the slayer,
>   And shall himself be slain;

I am not claiming that this is the highest order of poetry. It does not aim at that, and Matthew Arnold and others have done wrong in condemning it by that standard. But it is very good literature, and very good ballad. The lines on the cyclopæan walls of Volaterræ and the Arician lake where dwells

> The priest who slew the slayer
> And shall himself be slain

(the motto taken by Sir James Frazer for his *Golden Bough*), these and such-like words bit themselves into the minds of two generations of Englishmen. If the young no longer know the *Lays of Ancient Rome*, the loss is theirs.

The last of Macaulay's uses of geography in the *Lays*, is the end of *Prophecy of Capys*, giving a bird's-eye view of the world as known to the ancients, lying in the shadow of the crescent power of Republican Rome.

> Then where, o'er two bright havens,
>   The towers of Corinth frown;
> Where the gigantic King of Day
>   On his own Rhodes looks down;
> Where soft Orontes murmurs
>   Beneath the laurel shades;
> Where Nile reflects the endless length
>   Of dark-red colonnades;
> Where in the still deep water,
>   Sheltered from waves and blasts,
> Bristles the dusky forest
>   Of Byrsa's thousand masts;
> Where fur-clad hunters wander
>   Amidst the northern ice;
> Where through the sand of morning-land
>   The camel bears the spice;
> Where Atlas flings his shadow
>   Far o'er the western foam,
> Shall be great fear on all who hear
>   The mighty name of Rome.

Well, that is not bad, historically and geographically. But I will end the lecture with two pieces in a higher strain of poetry, but no less geographical, descriptive of travel in Italy, both by

Tennyson. Take first his lines on a visit to the Sirmio of
Catullus, the peninsula on the Lago di Garda:

> Row us out from Desenzano, to your Sirmione row!
> So they row'd, and there we landed—"O venusta Sirmio!"
> There to me thro' all the groves of olive in the summer glow,
> There beneath the Roman ruin where the purple flowers grow,
> Came that "Ave atque Vale" of the Poet's hopeless woe,
> Tenderest of Roman poets nineteen-hundred years ago,
> "Frater Ave atque Vale"—as we wander'd to and fro
> Gazing at the Lydian laughter of the Garda Lake below
> Sweet Catullus's all-but-island, olive-silvery Sirmio!

And last of all take a verse or two from that account of a tour
in Italy in the poem called *The Daisy*, which combines realism
of geographic truth and touristic experiences with lovely
poetic effects, largely resulting from Tennyson's delicate command of metre. After a description of sunlit scenes on the coast
of the riviera, and of the statues in the palaces of Genoa:

> A princely people's awful princes,
> The grave, severe Genovese of old,

we pass on to a bit of realism of Italian climate and travel:

> But when we crost the Lombard plain
> Remember what a plague of rain;
>   Of rain at Reggio, rain at Parma;
> At Lodi, rain, Piacenza, rain.
>
> And stern and sad (so rare the smiles
> Of sunlight) look'd the Lombard piles;
>   Porch-pillars on the lion resting,
> And sombre, old, colonnaded aisles,

leading up to Milan, and the distant view of Monte Rosa at
dawn seen by the poet from the roof of the Cathedral:

> O Milan, O the chanting quires,
> The giant windows' blazon'd fires,
>   The height, the space, the gloom, the glory!
> A mount of marble, a hundred spires!

I climb'd the roofs at break of day;
Sun-smitten Alps before me lay.
  I stood among the silent statues,
And statued pinnacles, mute as they.

How faintly-flush'd, how phantom-fair,
Was Monte Rosa, hanging there
  A thousand shadowy-pencill'd valleys
And snowy dells in a golden air.

Such can be the aids of geography to poets.

IV[1]

I WANT to begin this lecture by saying a few words about
the relations of history and fiction on their meeting ground
in the historical novel or play. What rights, if any, has
historical truth in historical fiction? I do not think it is possible
to lay down any precise rules, but perhaps some general
principles might be agreed upon, or at least discussed. The
question is not unimportant, because many people read very
few history books and get their ideas of history from fiction,
as Marlborough said he did from Shakespeare's historical
plays. Now it is undesirable that fundamentally false ideas
of the people and events of the past should be propagated
through fiction. And conversely fiction often serves a very
useful purpose in spreading true ideas about the past. This
purpose is no doubt subsidiary to the artistic and pleasure-
giving purposes of the historical novel or play, but those
primary purposes will I think be better subserved when the
history is true. For example, Tolstoi's *War and Peace* is a great
historical novel, gaining much in interest by the true picture
it gives of a bygone state of Russian society, and losing something by the false picture it gives of Napoleon as an unimportant
puppet. Even as a work of art the picture of the puppet
Napoleon fails, because it carries no conviction.

History, then, has some rights of its own in historical fiction.
What are they, and what are their limits?

Now the first principle I would suggest is a negative one,
that the novelist or playwright ought not to falsify a real
historical character, more especially by denigration. Sir Walter
Scott was far above this fault of libelling the dead. For example,
though his sympathies were Cavalier, his Cromwell in *Wood-
stock* was the first attempt since Oliver's death, to draw a true
picture of the real man.

[1] Parts of this Lecture first appeared in *The Book of the P.E.N.* for 1950.

But I will give a case of the sort of denigration to which I object. A good many years ago I saw on the London stage a play about Clive. In order further to exalt Clive, who surely stands high enough without such supports, the play misrepresented his faithful naval coadjutor, Admiral Watson, as a drunkard, a coward and a man altogether mean and hateful. The reason for this was that Admiral Watson quite rightly refused to join in signing the sham treaty to deceive Omichand, and Clive therefore had Watson's signature forged on to the document. With the *Dictionary of National Biography*, I think that it 'is impossible to offer any defence of this transaction', which stands in strong contrast to the general nobility of Clive's life and actions. The play, which might have avoided the incident altogether, chose to offer a defence by misrepresenting the whole situation and object of the false treaty, and in doing so it grossly misrepresented the character of the Admiral. It is quite right that libels on the dead are not actionable, for, if they were, who would dare to write history? But this legal immunity makes it a special duty of authors not to defame the dead, who have no protection.

Another negative principle which I think should be observed, is not to alter any important and well-known historical fact in its broad outlines. Minor alterations of fact and date are permissible and necessary in an historical novel or play, because history as it actually takes place is usually a confused and inartistic jumble of events, and requires manipulation for the artistic purposes of fiction. But there are limits. I remember seeing with dismay a film about the Armada, which had otherwise considerable merit, reaching its climax when the Spanish fleet was represented as being set on fire and burnt to the waterline by our fireships off Calais, whereas every Englishman knows that the Spaniards cut their cables in panic and ran north to their ultimate destruction by other elements than fire. Similarly, Schiller makes Joan of Arc die from wounds in battle! One result of such alterations in the broad and well-known outlines of historical fact, is that the spectator or reader cannot pretend to himself that he believes the rest of the film, play or story. The "illusion of reality" is destroyed.

Of course there is a very wide margin of debatable land and no rigid rule can be laid down, because it is a question of degree and a question of particular cases. Some dates and minor facts of Napoleon's career are altered by St. George Saunders (David Pilgrim) in his excellent novels about the Great Man; he acknowledges the alterations and they do not destroy credibility. Sir Walter Scott, the father of the historical novel, sometimes to my thinking took too large liberties of this sort, as when he brought Shakespeare into *Kenilworth* as a grown man at the time of Amy Robsart's death, which took place several years before he was born. This telescopes the two ends of Elizabeth's reign, which were very different one from the other. And the latter part of *Anne of Geierstein*, not a good novel at best, is utterly spoilt by the juggling with facts about King René and Queen Margaret which destroys the credibility that is maintained so consistently in the great Scottish novels. Sir Walter took fewer liberties with Scottish history than with English and French, and that is a minor reason why the Scottish novels are the best. If he had loved English and French history as he loved Scottish history he would not have played such tricks with them.

In Thackeray's historical novel of *Esmond*, which has caught the Queen Anne atmosphere wonderfully, the author introduced as the climax of the book a purely imaginary visit of the Old Pretender to England. It did not happen; but as it is supposed to be a secret visit of which the world never knew, it does not do crude violence to well-known historical fact; it remains therefore artistically credible and adds immensely to the interest of the book.

The historical novelist can usually avoid this problem of altering the facts and personalities of history by confining himself to fictitious incidents and characters, but he has still to get the social atmosphere and the habits of the age right, or he will cause as much offence to the historical ear as by a misrepresentation of famous people or events. Conan Doyle's

Rodney Stone and *Brigadier Gerard*, Stanley Weyman's *Ovington's Bank* and *Chippinge*, and in our own day C. S. Forester's *Hornblower* series and books on the Peninsular War are written with real knowledge of the period, and by the use of fictitious persons and events give us credible and stirring pictures of warfare in the days of Napoleon, and of society, banking and politics in the days of George and William IV. The main plot and persons being fictitious but historically credible, the occasional appearance in the wings of real characters like the Regent, Nelson, Napoleon and Brougham can be made appetizing morsels. The value of the stories is greatly enhanced by their historical interest, but this would not be so if these authors did not know well the period of the past on which they let their imagination play.

The English historical novelists whom I have just mentioned, in dealing with the Napoleonic and post-Napoleonic period, were concerned with an epoch only a century or so before their own time. And Sir Walter's and Stevenson's Scottish novels had the same advantage. A great part of their value lies in their historic interest; but the language and ways of thought of the Scots in *Rob Roy* and *Guy Mannering*, in *Kidnapped* and *The Master of Ballantrae* sufficiently resemble the language and ways of thought of the Scots known as contemporaries to Sir Walter and Stevenson, and therefore they and their speech are alive and real. For similar reasons Hardy's *Trumpet Major* succeeds as an historical novel; Hardy used his familiar understanding of the peasant population of Dorset, together with the local stories of the Napoleonic period that he had heard from them in his boyhood, just as Scott used his recollection of Jacobite and other old-world stories when he wrote *Waverley or 'tis Sixty Years since*.

To my thinking, the peculiar merit of Monty James's *Ghost Stories of an Antiquary* is not the ghosts and horrors themselves, but the subtle and learned reproduction of the thought, language and customs, especially in clerical circles, of various decades in the Eighteenth and Nineteenth Centuries, each carefully distinguished from the others—for example in the two parts of *The Residence in Whitminster*, *The Stalls of Barchester Cathedral*, and the *Episode in Cathedral History*. My point here is that even Monty James could not have produced these delightful effects, if he had thrown his stories back into the Sixteenth or earlier centuries, whose folk cannot be as vivid and familiar even to an Antiquary.

Indeed if the historical novel deals with a period two hundred years or more before the time of writing, the author's difficulties are very great. The language and habits of thought of the Middle Ages were so different from our own that even a mediæval scholar would find it difficult to reproduce them at once vividly and faithfully in fiction.

As regards language, this difficulty is faced, but not I think overcome, either by making mediæval folk talk modern English, or by the use of "tushery", as Stevenson himself called the language he employed so freely in *The Black Arrow*. 'Tush, good fellow bend me your bow shrewdly.' And it is perhaps equally difficult to understand and reproduce mediæval habits of thought. Nevertheless there have been some good novels recently written about the Middle Ages. Evan John's *Crippled Splendour* is a fine book and reproduces the atmosphere of the early Fifteenth Century with credibility.

And I confess that, in spite of the "tushery", I think Stevenson in *The Black Arrow* used his study of the Paston Letters and other historical sources to produce a vivid picture of the real social and political habits and the methods of warfare of the Wars of the Roses, just as his *Sire De Malétroit's Door* and *A Lodging for the Night* illuminate brightly the same epoch in France. It is true that the heroes and heroines of those Stevensonian tales are merely Nineteenth-century romantic conventions, in little relation to the mediæval mind, but the external picture of society and manners, and some of the other characters like Sir Daniel Brackley and Villon himself have real historical value.

For indeed a work of fiction may have historical value in one way and none at all in another. It may be impossible to reproduce the language used by people in the remote past; it may be difficult to understand their ways of thought and motives for action. And yet by dint of historical study it may be possible for the novelist to represent the externals of their social customs and ways of acting in peace and in war. A picture can be painted as it were in two dimensions. But the historical novelist who deals with comparatively recent times has a much greater chance of working from the inside as well as from the outside of his characters. It is not therefore surprising that the very greatest historical novels, Sir Walter's best, Stevenson's *Master of Ballantrae* and *Weir of Hermiston*, Tolstoi's *War and Peace* and Conrad's *Rover* are placed in periods not very far back in time.

I hope I am not dogmatizing on this extremely difficult and complicated subject, which is so much a question of fine shades and personal opinion. I don't know any subject connected with literature that could be more difficult, for history and fiction are clean different things. It may be said they agree as well as fire and water. Is not the phrase "historical fiction" a contradiction in terms? Yet it is an important branch of literature, particularly in our time. The complications and subtleties of the question are all the greater because there are different kinds of historical fiction, aiming at and requiring different degrees of historical reality, and we must judge them each by a different law.

For example, some of the best things in our literature are fantasies, placed indeed in an historical setting, but not demanding the degree of pretended belief on the part of the reader aimed at by the historical novels which I have so far been discussing. Take Peacock's *Maid Marian*. It is pure fantasy and fun, as much as *As You Like It*. It takes indeed the form of an historical tale, with Richard I as one of its characters. But in fact who cares about the historical possibility of it? It makes no claim on our belief in its reality, not so much for example as *Ivanhoe* which deals with the same period and subject, but in a different spirit. The historical errors in *Ivanhoe* are often discussed, but who would discuss the historical errors in *Maid Marian*? Peacock has merely taken a mediæval scene and the

Robin Hood ballads for a frolic of early Nineteenth-century laughter and poetry. It need be no more historically accurate than Gilbert and Sullivan's *Yeoman of the Guard*. Indeed the songs in *Maid Marian*, the best things in a delightful book, make no pretence whatever to be mediæval songs. They are woodland songs of all time:

> The bramble, the bramble, the bonny forest bramble,
>   Doth make a jest
>   Of silken vest,
> That will through greenwood scramble:
> The bramble, the bramble, the bonny forest bramble
>
> For the slender beech and the sapling oak
>   That grow by the shadowy rill,
> You may cut down both at a single stroke,
>   You may cut down which you will.
>
> But this you must know, that as long as they grow,
>   Whatever change may be,
> You never can teach either oak or beech
>   To be aught but a greenwood tree.

Even Friar Tuck's song as he guides King Richard and Maid Marian to the woodland repast of venison makes no antiquarian pretences:

> When the wind blows, when the wind blows
> From where under buck the dry log glows,
>   What guide can you follow,
>   O'er break and o'er hollow,
> So true as a ghostly, ghostly nose?

And the same may be said of Peacock's *Misfortunes of Elphin*. It also is a *fantasia*, not an historical novel. Who cares whether or not there ever were such Welshmen in prehistoric times? The War-song of Dinas Vawr does not raise the question whether Dinas Vawr or Ednyfed King of Dyfed ever existed:

> The mountain sheep are sweeter,
> But the valley sheep are fatter;
> We therefore deemed it meeter
> To carry off the latter.

We made an expedition;
We met a host and quelled it;
We forced a strong position,
And killed the men who held it.

On Dyfed's richest valley,
Where herds of kine were browsing,
We made a mighty sally,
To furnish our carousing.
Fierce warriors rushed to meet us;
We met them, and o'erthrew them:
They struggled hard to beat us;
But we conquered them, and slew them.

We brought away from battle,
And much their land bemoaned them,
Two thousand head of cattle,
And the head of him that owned them:
Ednyfed, king of Dyfed,
His head was borne before us;
His wine and beasts supplied our feasts,
And his overthrow, our chorus.

But now that we have admitted that there are at least two
kinds of historical fiction, we have, as the civil servants say,
"opened a very wide door". Why should there not be historical
plays and novels of an infinite variety of kinds, each with a
special relation of its own to the facts of history?

Bernard Shaw's plays, for instance, on Charles II, Julius
Cæsar and Joan of Arc. Are they fantasies or historical
dramas? Anything Bernard Shaw writes is in part a fantasia,
in part realism, and in part a propagandist essay. And this
remains true of his historical plays. As regards the amount of
historical credibility required for their full enjoyment, they seem
to me to stand half-way between *Maid Marian* and *Waverley*.

Mr. Thornton Wilder has tried his very able hand at
historical fiction dealing with the Græco-Roman civilization.
It lies so far back in time that no question of language arises:
no one would attempt any form of "tushery" to represent

Greek or Latin speech; the characters must frankly talk and write modern English. But the difficulty of understanding their minds and motives would be great even for a classical scholar.

Nevertheless, I thought Mr. Thornton Wilder's *Women of Andros* an artistic success. His fine imaginative and sympathetic qualities had free play on Andros, for they had not to be fitted into any known set of historical facts. An island society, far from the great world, had been wisely chosen and the tale kept clear of real historical characters and events.

For converse reasons I cared less for his *Ides of March*. In it a number of very famous historical men and women are made to speak for themselves in their letters. Moreover, Mr. Wilder has transposed at will their dates and their relations to one another. There is no deception, for in the Preface he points out that he has done so, defending it on the ground that: 'Historical reconstruction is not among the primary aims of this work. It may be called a fantasia on certain events and persons of the last days of the Roman Republic.' Now this would be valid if the "fantasia" were really fantastic, like Peacock's work. But, to me at least, the book reads like a realistic study of a number of historic persons and events. And for this reason I regret the loss of "credibility" due to the author's alteration of well-known facts. I do not say this dogmatically, for it is only my own reaction, and other readers may feel differently.

I have spoken in a previous lecture of Kipling's *Puck of Pook's Hill* and *Rewards and Fairies*. They stand half-way between the historical fantasia and the historical novel, half fairy story, half realism. Kipling's imagination peoples the English countryside with the dead of long ago, far more alive than the living, so that the question of their historical likelihood pales in the light of so much creative power. A book of the school of *Puck of Pook's Hill* is John Buchan's *Path of the King*, his best historical romance to my thinking, ending up with an imaginative picture of President Lincoln of real beauty and truth.

To sum up, there are so many different kinds of historical fiction that it is no use trying to lay down general rules about adherence to historical fact, which shall be equally applicable to all cases. But this discussion may perhaps have elicited some useful considerations.

Both as a professional historian and as a layman loving letters, I have always believed that history and literature cannot without great loss be separated. Specialization of studies is essential, but it has its dangers. There must be professional historians and professional students of literature. But they should not lose sight of each other's fields, and they have, or should have, much common ground of reading. On the whole, students of literature lose sight of history less often than professional historians lose sight of literature. The reason is obvious: for the student of literature cannot neglect the past, since most of his work concerns writers of times gone by; not only their individual lives but the mental climate in which they lived must be known to him before he can fully appreciate their writings or rightly judge the importance of what they did in their day. As I have said, I think the school of English at Cambridge is in this sense closely and consciously wedded to history.

As to the general reader, the layman loving letters, it is utterly impossible for him to draw a line between history and literature. He reads them on the same page and does not ask himself which he is reading. To take the most obvious example, when the Bible was the normal reading of all classes, and the classics of the educated class, the nation may be said to have been studying history and literature together, and largely for that reason it was, in many respects a finer education of mind and imagination than anything we are likely to get again so widely spread. In our modern age the general reader still has the Bible, and a few of the educated still have the classics, available if they care to use them. And beyond that a wide field of interest and delight lies open to all, where each can make his choice and take his pleasure, in English books that are at once history and literature. If for the moment we leave poetry and fiction out of account, Boswell's *Johnson* heads the list. Is it history or is it literature? Who shall determine, and

6

who cares? Of the same genre are Horace Walpole's letters, Gibbon's autobiography, Byron's letters, much of Swift and Addison. And earlier times left us Bacon's essays, Milton's *Areopagitica*, Bunyan's *Pilgrim's Progress*, and the incomparable political writings of Halifax. For the enjoyment of such great books only a little knowledge of history is needed, but the more historical knowledge we have the more we enjoy them. There are indeed scores of other delightful books, flotsam and jetsam of England's past. To name only a few examples: the memoirs of Madame D'Arblay, of Greville, of Creevey, Lockhart's *Scott*, Sydney Smith's *Plymley Letters*, the poetry of *The Anti-Jacobin*, Hazlitt's *Spirit of the Age*, the speeches of Disraeli and Macaulay, the Autobiographies of Lord Herbert of Cherbury and of John Stuart Mill, Johnson's *Lives of the Poets*, Thomas Bewick's Memoirs, Borrow's *Lavengro*, Kinglake's *Eothen*—the list can be extended indefinitely and you can class them all either as materials for history or as literature. No country, not even France, is richer in such books.

One immortal writer, Edmund Burke, a man often faulty in conduct and in opinion, but sometimes very wise and always very great, has left us writings which, being past politics have now become history, but which are also, by all the gods, literature. Listen to this, from his Speech on the Conciliation of the American Colonies:

> But to clear up my ideas on this subject,—a revenue from America transmitted hither. Do not delude yourselves: you can never receive it, no not a shilling. . . . For that service, for all service, whether of revenue, trade or empire, my trust is in America's interest in the British Constitution. My hold of the colonies is in the close affection which grows from common names, from kindred blood, from similar privileges, and equal protection. These are ties which, though light as air, are as strong as links of iron. Let the colonies always keep the idea of their civil rights associated with your government,—they will cling and grapple to you, and no force under heaven will be of power to tear them from their allegiance. But let it be once understood that your government may be one thing and their privileges another, that these two things may exist without any mutual relation,—the

cement is gone, the cohesion is loosened, and everything hastens to decay and dissolution. As long as you have the wisdom to keep the sovereign authority of this country as the sanctuary of liberty, the sacred temple consecrated to our common faith, wherever the chosen race and sons of England worship freedom, they will turn their faces towards you. The more they multiply, the more friends you will have; the more ardently they love liberty, the more perfect will be their obedience. Slavery they can have anywhere. It is a weed that grows in every soil. They may have it from Spain, they may have it from Prussia. But, until you become lost to all feeling of your true interest and your natural dignity, freedom they can have from none but you. This is the commodity of price, of which you have the monopoly. . . . Magnanimity in politics is not seldom the truest wisdom; and a great empire and little minds go ill together.

Another way to state my theme is to say that everything that records the past of man is History, although professional historians only deal with certain aspects thereof, and other specialists with other parts. History, thus defined, is the House in which are found side by side past politics, war, economics, law and society; past religion, science, art and architecture; the poetry and literature of the past and much else besides. They are all in close relation to one another in our memory, as they were in the actual lives of our ancestors. All these aspects of life in the past must indeed be studied separately, but they are all inextricably linked, constantly reacting upon and altering one another. They are parts of the great picture of the past of man, which is all the dearer to us now that we are no longer so well satisfied with the prospect of his present and of his future. They ought all to be at the back of the consciousness of every student, however deeply immersed he may rightly be in his own particular section of the whole.

Some history books, written in English, are literature as well as history. Clarendon, Gibbon, Carlyle, Macaulay, Maitland with his unique style and unique mind—and from overseas Parkman—are leading cases, and there are many more. But I do not think the Clark Lectures are a proper place to discuss them, for these are not lectures on History. I turn rather to the uses of historical knowledge in enabling us more fully to understand and love English literature. Our poets have indeed written a great deal of their very best for which historical knowledge is not required. But they have nearly all of them written some poems which can be more fully appreciated if we know something of the historical circumstances which produced them or to which they incidentally refer.

Take, for example, Clough's *Amours de Voyage*. To my mind it is the best of his long poems, though *The Bothie* runs it close. Together they have found a use for the hexameter in English which no other poet has approached. Now of course the central theme of *Amours de Voyage*, the young Englishman who cannot make up his mind in time about the young lady, needs no historical comment. But the poem gains much in interest by being set in Rome during the months of its defence by Garibaldi in 1849. And a little knowledge of that strange and picturesque episode in history adds to our enjoyment of the whole.

> Rome is fallen, I hear, the gallant Medici taken,
> Noble Manara slain, and Garibaldi has lost *il Moro*;
> Rome is fallen; and fallen, or falling, heroical Venice.
> I, meanwhile, for the loss of a single small chit of a girl, sit
> Moping and mourning here,—for her, and myself much smaller.
> Whither depart the souls of the brave that die in the battle,
> Die in the lost, lost fight, for the cause that perishes with them?
> Are they upborne from the field on the slumberous pinions of angels
> Unto a far-off home, where the weary rest from their labour,
> And the deep wounds are healed, and the bitter and burning moisture
> Wiped from the generous eyes? or do they linger, unhappy,
> Pining, and haunting the grave of their by-gone hope and endeavour?
>
> All declamation, alas! though I talk, I care not for Rome nor
> Italy; feebly and faintly, and but with the lips, can lament the
> Wreck of the Lombard youth, and the victory of the oppressor.
> Whither depart the brave?—God knows: I certainly do not.

And Clough's short poem on *Peschiera* means little unless the reader knows that the Italians fought for their freedom there and failed.

The first part of George Meredith's *Vittoria*, down to the end of the scene in the opera house at Milan, is one of the finest of the many fine things written in English about the Risorgimento. After that point, the book goes to pieces, its strong current lost and straying in shallows, like "the shorn and parcell'd Oxus" in Arnold's poem, as so many of Meredith's novels tail off from his inability to tell a story straight through to its end.

The second chapter, the scene on Monte Motterone whence "you survey the Lombard plain", opens with the best description of Mazzini ever written, though Meredith never gives him any name except the Chief:

He was a man of middle stature, thin, and even frail, as he stood defined against the sky; with the complexion of the student, and the student's aspect. The attentive droop of his shoulders and head, the straining of the buttoned coat across his chest, the air as of one who waited and listened, which distinguished his figure, detracted from the promise of other than contemplative energy, until his eyes were fairly seen and felt. That is, until the observer became aware that those soft and large dark meditative eyes had taken hold of him. In them lay no abstracted student's languor, no reflex burning of a solitary lamp; but a quiet grappling force engaged the penetrating look. Gazing upon them, you were drawn in suddenly among the thousand whirring wheels of a capacious and a vigorous mind, that was both reasoning and prompt, keen of intellect, acting throughout all its machinery, and having all under full command; an orbed mind, supplying its own philosophy, and arriving at the sword-stroke by logical steps,—a mind much less supple than a soldier's; anything but the mind of a Hamlet. The eyes were dark as the forest's border is dark; not as the night is dark. Under favourable lights their colour was seen to be a deep rich brown, like the chestnut, or more like the hazel-edged sunset brown which lies upon our western rivers in the winter floods, when night begins to shadow them.

In my first lecture I quoted the praise bestowed by Matthew Arnold on Byron for the "fiery battle" which he waged against "the conservatism of the old impossible world". Though I do not agree with Arnold in placing Byron's political poetry above Shelley's lyrics, we must indeed put it very high. And it is better understood with the help of historical knowledge. The finest piece in this sort, perhaps, is *The Age of Bronze* with its lines on Napoleon at St. Helena, its attack on the Holy Alliance abroad and the governing classes at home. But how much more we appreciate it "with the aids of history" as Uncle Toby would have said. Let me quote the lines on the Czar Alexander as he was in 1823; the more you know of his person and his politics the more the lines strike home:

> Resplendent sight! Behold the coxcomb Czar,
> The autocrat of waltzes and of war!
> As eager for a plaudit as a realm,
> And just as fit for flirting as the helm;
> A Calmuck beauty with a Cossack wit,
> And generous spirit, when 'tis not frost-bit;
> Now half dissolving to a liberal thaw,
> But harden'd back whene'er the morning's raw;
> With no objection to true liberty,
> Except that it would make the nations free.
> How well the imperial dandy prates of peace!
> How fain, if Greeks would be his slaves, free Greece!
> How nobly gave he back the Poles their Diet,
> Then told pugnacious Poland to be quiet!

Or again, take the case of the poet Gray. Though I do not agree with Matthew Arnold in putting his lyrics above the *Elegy*, still if Arnold thought so, they must at least be very good indeed. But what would one make of *The Bard* and *The Installation Ode* if one had not at least a sound schoolboy knowledge of the Kings and Queens of England, their characters and fates. Another less well known poem of Gray's was evidently admired by Matthew Arnold, for he chose it for a place in his short selection of Gray's work in Ward's *Poets*. It is called an *Impromptu. Suggested by a view, in 1766, of the seat*

and ruins of a deceased nobleman, by Kingsgate, Kent. Though the
first Lord Holland was in fact still alive in 1766, it is an attack
on his political conduct, and a sneer at the sham ruins he had
erected round his rural retreat.

> Here mouldering fanes and battlements arise,
>   Turrets and arches nodding to their fall,
> Unpeopled monast'ries delude our eyes,
>   And mimic desolation covers all.
>
> "Ah!" said the sighing peer, "had Bute been true,
>   Nor Mungo's, Rigby's, Bradshaw's friendship vain,
> Far better scenes than these had blest our view,
>   And realis'd the beauties which we feign:
>
> "Purg'd by the sword, and purified by fire,
>   Then had we seen proud London's hated walls;
> Owls would have hooted in St. Peter's choir,
>   And foxes stunk and litter'd in St. Paul's."

You have to know more of the history of the period than is
told you in the notes even of learned editions of Gray, before
you can understand the extraordinary bitterness of these lines,
so unlike the placid temper of Gray, who, as his friend com-
plained, "never spoke out". Well he "speaks out" here against
Lord Holland. *Ira facit versus.* And if you want to know why,
if you want to know the political events that inspired the poem,
I refer you to the first chapter of my father's *Early Life of
Charles James Fox.*

Poems dealing in such detail with the politics of a bygone
age are of course exceptional, and the corpus of English poetry
can for the most part be understood and enjoyed without the
help of historical knowledge. But there are many different
degrees of comprehension. And the more we know about the
past, the more completely shall we understand and enjoy its
literature. The various aspects of the reaction of the French
Revolution and Napoleonic Wars on English politics, society
and thought form a background necessary not indeed for the

enjoyment but for the fullest understanding of Wordsworth, Coleridge, Scott, Byron and Shelley. A corresponding statement could be made about the history of our own revolutionary period in relation to Milton, Marvell and Dryden. The study of Shakespeare, into which our present age has so deeply and admirably advanced, is a study not only of the text of his plays but of the society and stagecraft of Elizabethan England. In the study of Chaucer and of the earlier Tudor poets the element of history is no less strong. In short, both for the student and for the general reader, it is impossible to draw a clear dividing line on one side of which all is history while on the other side all is literature.

Such is the conclusion to which this lecture has arrived. I will only add to it a rider. When I speak of history in this connection I should include a schoolboy knowledge of the myths and the heroes of ancient Greece and Rome; for our poets, from Chaucer and Gower to Matthew Arnold and Meredith, almost without exception used classical history and mythology as subjects to which they refer as common ground between themselves and their readers.

Literature, much more than either music or painting, produces its effects by reference to things known. The feeling of the reader about subjects referred to in poems often adds greatly, and is meant by the poet to add, to the feelings aroused by his own words. 'The glory that was Greece and the grandeur that was Rome' form a magazine inside our minds which our English poets love to set on fire. For example, on the dark Gothic platform at Elsinore after the mute appearance and disappearance of the ghost of Hamlet's father, Horatio suddenly exclaims:

> A mote it is to trouble the mind's eye.
> In the most high and palmy state of Rome,
> A little ere the mightiest Julius fell,
> The graves stood tenantless, and the sheeted dead
> Did squeak and gibber in the Roman streets.

* * *

And even the like precurse of fierce events
And prologue to the omen coming on—
Have heaven and earth together demonstrated
Unto our climatures and countrymen.

Now if we had never heard of Rome and of Julius Cæsar, this
wonderful passage would lose more than half its force. As it is,
even if we are not like Horatio "scholars", we all of us, including Bernardo and Marcellus to whom he addresses these
words, know enough to be raised, by the reference to "the
mightiest Julius" and "the most high and palmy state of
Rome", into an imaginative region which adds to the majestic
horror of the Ghost, who next moment re-enters to harrow us
with fear and wonder. In a sense those words are a "prologue"
to the whole play and its "fierce events".

And not only poetry but prose fiction thus often heightens
its effects by bringing the noblest type of imagination to light
up our historical knowledge. Take for instance *The Rover* of
Conrad. I do not say it is the greatest of his novels, though it
may be; at least I read it oftenest of all. It has the qualities
we find in his other books, and the characters of Peyrol and
Arlette could have been created by no other hand than
Conrad's. The whole book is as distinctive of him as *Lord Jim*.
Its fundamental greatness is therefore independent of its
historical setting. But it has the additional or incidental value
of playing most powerfully on our historical feeling about two
subjects that interest us all—the violences of the French
Revolution and the vigilance of Nelson and his men. The
frightful scenes of "the red fool fury" of the murderous mob
in Toulon are contrasted not only with the better French
patriotism of the steadfast Peyrol, but also with the disciplined
English seamen at watch off that coast, and the one brief
glimpse, restrained, subtle and strong, of Nelson himself.
As always, personal honour is what interests Conrad in human
beings, not their politics or their nationality. Peyrol and the
English seamen, though enemies, are all approved, for all are
honourable men. For the Jacobins he has no use, but his heart
is with loyal Frenchmen and loyal Englishmen, above all with

sailors. When England, through her merchant marine, made a conquest of the heart of Conrad, and enlisted his "imaginary forces" in the service of her language and literature, our country by the merits of her seamen won a thing of priceless value of which she may be for ever proud.

I mentioned earlier in this lecture, the position of Boswell's *Johnson* in our literature. It has indeed affected English thought and imagination to a supreme degree. My friend John Bailey, who like several other eminent critics wrote an excellent little book on Dr. Johnson, once told me a curious story, illustrative of the persistence of Johnson's popular fame. Some sixty years ago, as he was passing the cabmen's shelter in Piccadilly, he brushed close to two cabmen going into it for their midday meal, and overheard one say to the other, "As Dr. Johnson said, *There is nothing a man sees better than his dinner*." Bailey said he had never been able to find it in Boswell or elsewhere. Yet it is pure Johnson both in purport and in expression. The man who invented it, whether the cabman or another, was a true Johnsonian.

V

I SHALL begin this lecture by asking you to consider a very distinctive and local section of our poetic heritage, rightly described as the Border Ballads. Most of them, including many of the best, were written on the Scottish side, but some quite certainly in England, like *Chevy Chase*; and *The Death of Parcy Reed*, *Lamkin*, *The Fair Flower of Northumberland*, and *Fair Mary of Wallington* all tell of Northumbrian tragedies. The land that produced these Border Ballads, Scottish and English alike, was inhabited by lawless clans of peculiar social habits— the raid, the feud, the bringing of the fray—the same on both sides of the Cheviot ridge. The Mosstroopers of Liddesdale in Scotland and of North Tyne and Rede in England were much more like each other in life and thought than either were like the south English, and they had a ballad tradition in common equally distinct from that of the South; I will not call it a ballad *literature*, for most of it was passed on not in writing but through the mouths of men. It is impossible to identify the poets who composed this minstrelsy. Thomas the Rhymer of Erceldoune was a real person living in the Scottish borderland, but so far back in time, the Thirteenth Century, that he cannot be responsible for a single ballad in anything at all resembling its present form and language. The poem that tells of his famous jaunt with the Queen of Fairies was composed long after his death—how long no one knows.

As regards the date of the Ballads there is a wide margin. *The Battle of Otterburne* and *Chevy Chase* describe, the one correctly the other fancifully, a famous campaign and battle chronicled by Froissart and fought in the reign of Richard II; those two ballads were probably composed not long afterwards. On the other hand, *The Death of Parcy Reed* is an exact record of a feud murder on the fellside "high in Batinghope" in upper Redesdale, that actually took place as late as the reign of

85

Charles I; and *The Bonnie House of Airlie* tells of happenings in the Scottish wars of Argyle and Montrose. We have therefore a period of some three centuries during which the Border Ballads were being composed, generation after generation, and being moulded, doubtless by frequent changes, into their present form. For a long time, they were not written down or printed, but handed on by word of mouth, often sung or "soothed", sometimes to the fiddle, sometimes by milkmaids at their task:

> 'I've heard them lilting at our ewe milking
> Lassies a lilting before break of day.'

Gradually some of the ballads stole into print and became known to a wider and more distant audience. Addison, in *The Spectator*, writes that the English Ballad of *Chevy Chase*

> is the favourite ballad of the common people of England, and Ben Jonson used to say that he had rather have been the author of it than of all his works. Sir Philip Sidney in his Discourse of Poetry speaks of it in the following words: "I never heard the old song of Percy and Douglas that I found not my heart more moved than with a trumpet."

But this was exceptional. Most of the ballads, being of purely local interest, were known only to warriors in remote peel-towers or to shepherd folk secluded in the roadless dales of the Border. At length Bishop Percy in 1765 published his *Reliques of Ancient English Poetry*, which contained among much else a number of the Border Ballads that he had found in old MS. copies, chiefly I think of the later Seventeenth Century. Amongst them was the dialogue of the parricide with his guilty mother, which Bishop Percy printed in all the scaly horror of very old Scottish spelling, which I shall not reproduce, implying a pronunciation to which I will not pretend to do justice:

> "Why does your brand sae drop wi' blude,
> Edward, Edward?
> Why does your brand sae drop wi' blude,
> And why sae sad gang ye, O?"—

*　　　*　　　*

"O I hae kill'd my father dear,
    Mither, mither;
 O I hae kill'd my father dear,
    Alas, and wae is me, O!"

*   *   *

"And what will ye do wi' your tow'rs and your ha',
    Edward, Edward?
 And what will ye do wi' your tow'rs and your ha',
    That were sae fair to see, O?"—
"I'll let them stand till they doun fa',
    Mither, mither;
 I'll let them stand till they doun fa',
    For here never mair maun I be, O."

"And what will ye leave to your bairns and your wife,
    Edward, Edward?
 And what will ye leave to your bairns and your wife,
    When ye gang owre the sea, O?"—
"The warld's room: let them beg through life,
    Mither, mither:
 The warld's room: let them beg through life;
    For them never mair will I see, O."

"And what will ye leave to your ain mither dear,
    Edward, Edward?
 And what will ye leave to your ain mither dear,
    My dear son, now tell me, O?"—
"The curse of hell frae me sall ye bear,
    Mither, mither;
 The curse of hell frae me sall ye bear:
    Sic counsels ye gave to me, O!"

This tremendous piece of work frightened or puzzled the good
Bishop a little I think. He calls it "This curious song". A
curious song indeed! It must, in 1765, have given a jog to the
public brought up on Pope.

At the end of the century came the decisive act: young
Walter Scott penetrated into still roadless Liddesdale, and
collected ballads by word of mouth from his boon-companions,
the Dandie Dinmonts of the region. He gave these newfound

treasures to the world in 1802, in the first two volumes of *Minstrelsy of the Scottish Border*, the ancient fount whence his own modern greatness was to flow.

By Scott's time the Border was a peaceful and well-ordered land. Burns and the Bible, tempered by hard drinking, had succeeded the savage old "riding ballads", but fortunately enough of them were still remembered to repay the ardent search of antiquarians. Since then, there have been many editions of the Border Ballads, sometimes separately printed, more often intermingled with the ballads of mid and south England. The volume in which most of them are now most easily found is *The Oxford Book of Ballads*, so well selected and edited by Quiller Couch.

Now if you have read the Border Ballads there, or in *Percy's Reliques* or elsewhere, printed side by side with the ballad poetry of south England, you may perhaps feel, as I certainly feel, that much as we delight in the minstrelsy of the South, the Border Ballads contain more passages of really great poetry: and that they are more deeply tragic in feeling. Listen for example to the talk of *The Twa Corbies*:

> As I was walking all alane,
> I heard twa corbies making a mane:
> The tane unto the tither did say,
> "Whar sall we gang and dine the day?"
>
> "—In behint yon auld fail[1] dyke
> I wot there lies a new-slain knight;
> And naebody kens that he lies there
> But his hawk, his hound, and his lady fair.
>
> "His hound is to the hunting gane,
> His hawk to fetch the wild-fowl hame,
> His lady's ta'en anither mate,
> So we may mak' our dinner sweet.
>
> "Ye'll sit on his white hause[2]-bane
> And I'll pike out his bonny blue e'en:
> Wi'ae lock o' his gowden hair
> We'll theek our nest when it grows bare.

[1] fail = turf.   [2] hause = neck.

"Mony a one for him maks mane,
But nane sall ken whar he is gane:
O'er his white banes, when they are bare,
The wind sall blaw for evermair."

That sounds a deeper and more savage note of human destiny than the corresponding south English ballad, *The Three Ravens*, treating the same subject but with a gentler melancholy.

None of the Border Ballads are as charming as our *Nut-brown Maid* of the south-English greenwood, but there are some that are greater and many that are more terrible. If the Nut-brown Maid had been a Border lass, she would not have won her outlaw earl at the end, but would have seen him "waver with the wind" on the gallows tree. And the same may be said of that lucky *Bailiff's Daughter of Islington*. To assume the part of lover in a Border Ballad is a more desperate undertaking. When her brother determines to burn Scottish Lady Maisry for loving an Englishman too well, Lord William rides up too late to do anything but burn her whole family in revenge, and throw himself into the flames at the end.

The Robin Hood ballads, of which Q. gives a large collection in the Oxford book, are rollicking fun. On the Border, such laughter was not heard. The lives of folk there were too grim and bloody. They were constantly engaged in three several kinds of warfare. First, invasion of England by Scotland or of Scotland by England—whether royal armies were engaged as at Flodden, or only a few score cattle-raiders invading the enemy kingdom, as in the ballad of *Jamie Telfer*, an exact description of the usual procedure of a raid across the border with its outcome of deadly battle. Secondly, the raids of border thieves on their own side of the national frontier: the men of Liddesdale in Scotland and the men of Redesdale and North Tyne in England formed outlaw communities paying obedience to neither King, and living by raids upon those of their own fellow-countrymen who dwelt in richer and slightly more law-abiding lands in Scotland and Northumberland indifferently. The third sort of war along the Border was that of family against family: these private feuds lay not only between one clan and another in the dales of the outlaws, but between the keepers of castles and peel-towers in the more settled regions, who at least outwardly acknowledged the distant Kings in London or in Edinburgh, but in fact obeyed either Percy or Douglas, or each man his own fierce will.

The Border life, at any rate in its most highly developed form in the outlaw valleys of Liddesdale, Rede and North Tyne, had no set object, no political or social end to attain. It was a life good or bad in itself alone. These people have left nothing but their ballads, which have made their meaningless and wicked ways interesting for all time. Their life was a game with Death, in which each in turn was sure to pay forfeit at last; it was played according to certain rules of clan and family honour, varied and crossed by lovers' passions. All classes of a sparse population lived together on terms not of equality but of feudal familiarity, and all joined in this game with Death, and relished it as the poetry and breath of life. Their ballads are nearly all tragic, and the best ballads are the most tragic. Something grand and inevitable, like the doom impending over the Lion Gate of Mycenæ, broods over each of these stone castles and peel-towers built high "upon the bent", or in the wilder parts rude forts of mighty oak trunks cased in turf. It was as savage a society as that of Homer or of the Vikings, though contemporaneous with the high civilization of Shakespeare's England down south. The two very different types of poetry produced at the same time in the one island were the outcome of two very different social scenes.

I do not mean that brutal or tragic conditions of life always produce great poems. Our own Total Wars and their legacy have done more to silence song than to inspire it. But these sparse inhabiters of moorland fell, cut off from the great world beyond, and living before the days of science and locomotion, did in fact produce not only murders and frays but great poetry to describe them.

Helen of Kirconnell is the old Border ballad from which young Tennyson long afterwards drew the idea for his own *Oriana*.

I wish I were where Helen lies,
Night and day on me she cries;
O that I were where Helen lies,
　　On fair Kirconnell lea;

Curst be the heart that thought the thought,
And curst the hand that fired the shot,
When in my arms burd Helen dropt,
　　And died to succour me!

*　　*　　*

As I went down the water side,
None but my foe to be my guide,
None but my foe to be my guide,
　　On fair Kirconnell lea ;

I lighted down my sword to draw,
I hackèd him in pieces sma',
I hackèd him in pieces sma',
　　For her sake that died for me.

*　　*　　*

I wish I were where Helen lies!
Night and day on me she cries;
And I am weary of the skies,
　　For her sake that died for me.

Thus the Border Ballads show their mastery of the tragic
note in events of the real human life of their day, but they are
no less powerful in the realm of fairy, of magic and of the eerie.
The ride of Thomas the Rhymer with the Queen of Elfland
I mentioned above :

O they rade on, and farther on,
　　And they waded rivers abune the knee;
And they saw neither sun nor moon,
　　But they heard the roaring of the sea.

It was mirk, mirk night, there was nae starlight,
　　They waded thro' red blude to the knee;
For a' the blude that's shed on the earth
　　Rins through the springs o' that countrie.

7

And in another Ballad, the same Queen of Fairies steals a young
mother from a farm to be Elphin Nourice (Elf nurse) to the
little Prince of Fairies. The poor woman hears out of fairyland
a noise of the dear world she has left, and remembers her own
son.

"I heard a cow low, a bonnie cow low,
    An' a cow low doun in yon glen;
Lang, lang, will my young son greet,
    Or his mither bid him come ben.

"I heard a cow low, a bonnie cow low,
    An' a cow low doun in yon fauld;
Lang, lang, will my young son greet,
    Or his mither take him frae cauld.

"Waken, Queen of Elfan,
    An' hear your Nourice moan."
"O moan ye for your meat,
    Or moan ye for your fee,
Or moan ye for the ither bounties
    That ladies are wont to gie?"

"I moan na for my meat,
    Nor yet for my fee,
But I mourn for Christen land—
    It's there I fain would be."

One of the most charming of these eerie ballads is *The Wife
of Usher's Well*, the mother who has lost her three sons and
disturbs their peace in the next world by her imprecations:

"I wish the wind may never cease,
    Nor fashes in the flood,
Till my three sons come hame to me
    In earthly flesh and blood!"

It fell about the Martinmas,
    When nights are lang and mirk,
The carline wife's three sons came hame,
    And their hats were o' the birk.

It neither grew in syke[1] nor ditch,
  Nor yet in ony sheugh[2];
But at the gates o' Paradise
  That birk grew fair eneugh.

A Lyke-Wake Dirge is a powerful and uncouth expression of
the popular superstitions of the Middle Ages, as distinct from
the higher flights of cultivated Italian and French Catholicism.
It is sung by the borderers by the bedside of a man whose soul
is passing on its journey to the next world.

This ae nighte, this ae nighte,
  —*Every nighte and alle,*
Fire and fleet and candle-lighte,
  And Christe receive thy saule.

When thou from hence away art past,
  —*Every nighte and alle,*
To Whinny-muir thou com'st at last:
  And Christe receive thy saule.

If ever thou gavest hosen and shoon,
  —*Every nighte and alle,*
Sit thee down and put them on:
  And Christe receive thy saule.

If hosen and shoon thou ne'er gav'st nane
  —*Every nighte and alle,*
The whinnes sall prick thee to the bare bane;
  And Christe receive thy saule.

I have not time to quote from *Clerk Sanders*; moreover it
ought to be read as a whole. In that ballad the two notes of
the tragic and the eerie are blended; each in perfection. In
the fertility of its imagination clothed in the stark simplicity
of its words, *Clerk Sanders* is one of the greatest poems in our
language, though no one will ever know who wrote it.

Indeed these Border Ballads raise a question analogous to
the vexed Homeric question, though in this case we have even
fewer data than the disputants over the unity of Homer. Some

[1] syke = marsh.   [2] sheugh = trench.

of the Border Ballads, or at least some of their verses, are inspired by what we call poetic genius. But we cannot tell how many minstrels of genius there were, whether they were all of one region or of one generation of men. The Border Ballads as a whole spread from the end of the Fourteenth to the middle of the Seventeenth Century. But are their highest qualities the work of a few specially gifted minstrels at a particular time? We do not know. But in any case that unlettered and lawless population as a whole must have had much more feeling for poetry than the population of today.

There is, fortunately, a great body of south English Ballads, composed during a period stretching from the later Middle Ages down to the end of the Nineteenth Century. Indeed as late as fifty years ago humble folk occasionally wrote ballads on events of the day according to the old tradition. I have seen a genuine ballad about a fire, the last verse of which begins "O London County Council". But even in Tudor times, when the tradition was at its best (as in the *Nut-brown Maid*) the south English ballad did not often touch the poetic heights of the best Border Ballads. Yet even when a ballad is slightly absurd to our sophisticated modern ears, it is nearly always well worth reading. The four Elizabethan ballads about the war with Spain are old favourites: *Brave Lord Willoughbey*, *The Winning of Cales* (Cadiz), *Mary Ambree* and *The Spanish Lady's Love*, a beautiful poem. Unlike Dr. Johnson, Macaulay loved our ballad literature, old and new, good and bad; he bought it on the streets from still surviving ballad-mongers, and sought it out in the bookstalls with indefatigable zest. He was particularly delighted and amused by *Brave Lord Willoughbey* with its spirited account of a battle in the Low Countries:

> "Stand to it, noble pikemen,
>   And look you round about:
> And shoot you right, you bow-men,
>   And we will keep them out.
> You musquet and calliver men,
>   Do you prove true to me:

I'le be the formost man in fight,"
Says brave Lord Willoughbèy.

And above all he rejoiced in the very practical finale in the
true ballad style:

To the souldiers that were maimed
And wounded in the fray,
The queen allowed a pension
Of fifteen pence a day;
And from all costs and charges
She quit and set them free:
And this she did all for the sake
Of brave Lord Willoughbèy.

It was a fine gesture on the part of Queen Elizabeth I, but from
my knowledge of that great monarch's financial exigencies and
policies, I shrewdly doubt whether the poor men's pensions
were ever paid. Brave Lord Willoughbey himself had been
most scandalously ill paid and ill supplied, and came back
from his fine service in the Low Countries a ruined man. Let
us hope he thought the ballad-writers, whose favourite he was,
made up to him what he had sacrificed for Queen and country.

To return to the Border Ballads, for a last word. Scott wrote
in imitation of them his *Proud Maisie*, which some have considered the best of his many short poems.

Proud Maisie is in the wood,
Walking so early;
Sweet Robin sits on the bush,
Singing so rarely.

"Tell me, thou bonny bird,
When shall I marry me?"
—"When six braw gentlemen
Kirkward shall carry ye."

"Who makes the bridal bed,
Birdie, say truly?"
—"The grey-headed sexton
That delves the grave duly.

"The glow-worm o'er grave and stone
Shall light thee steady;
The owl from the steeple sing
Welcome, proud lady!"

I should like to say something more about Scott, as the author of the Waverley novels. Fifty-five years ago I was walking amid the ruins of Kenilworth Castle, where I encountered another "picturesque tourist", a dear old lady who amused me by exclaiming "I find that the Wizard of the North has lost none of the magic of his power". Even then the form of the remark seemed to come from a bygone age. And by now I fear that Scott has lost all his magic for many people, and much of it for all. Indeed I think he is now underestimated. Proper distinction is now too seldom made, dividing what is commonplace and ephemeral in his work, from what is great and enduring. This difference answers roughly (not of course exactly) to the difference between his English and his Scottish prose. Similarly, with regard to his characters, his Englishmen, and his gentlefolk even when Scottish, are usually weak and conventional; this is particularly true of many of his heroes and heroines (Diana Vernon always excepted and even she sometimes talks like the drawing room parrot). It is the middle and lower classes of Scotland who supply almost all Sir Walter's great creations.

My friend Mr. Morgan Forster, in his Clark Lectures for 1927, better known to the world as the volume entitled *Some Aspects of the Novel*, tells us that "provincialism" is a serious fault in a critic (p. 17). I agree. Only how shall we define "provincialism"? He seems to me himself to suffer from an English provincialism when he despises the Scottish vernacular part of our literature. In *Aspects of the Novel* he condemns Sir Walter's Scottish novels wholesale. He does not care for the language, character and humour of Dandie Dinmont, Meg Merrilies, Andrew Fairservice, Jeanie Deans and all that galaxy of Scottish folk. To me they seem at least as real and living as the characters of Dickens. They are not what

Mr. Forster usefully defines as "flat" characters (except, I will grant to him, Caleb Balderstone). They are real men and women and are seen "in the round". And their Scottish talk, full of the salt of life, is amusing and powerful. But the only merit that Mr. Forster can see in Sir Walter is that he can tell an exciting story. His prose he despises, his character drawing he does not even discuss except in the case of Caleb Balderstone, which as I say I will grant him.

It may seem an impertinence that I should openly differ from Mr. Forster on a subject connected with fiction, an art in which he is perhaps our greatest living master. And many of his essays in *Two Cheers for Democracy* seem to me first-rate literary criticism. I would not therefore for a moment traverse the general lines of the argument and analysis set out in *Some Aspects of the Novel*. Mr. Forster is a high authority; I am only a layman loving letters. But as I think he has a blind spot about the Scottish characters and language of Sir Walter's best novels, I will venture to join issue with him on that point and on that alone.

First I will read what he says.

Who shall tell us a story?

Sir Walter Scott, of course.

Scott is a novelist over whom we shall violently divide. For my own part I do not care for him, and find it difficult to understand his continued reputation. His reputation in his day—that is easy to understand. There are important historical reasons for it, which we should discuss if our scheme was chronological. But when we fish him out of the river of time and set him to write in that circular room with the other novelists, he presents a less impressive figure. He is seen to have a trivial mind and a heavy style. He cannot construct. He has neither artistic detachment nor passion, and how can a writer who is devoid of both, create characters who will move us deeply?

*   *   *

His fame is due to two causes. In the first place, many of the elder generation had him read aloud to them when they were young; he is entangled with happy sentimental memories, with holidays in or residence in Scotland. They love him indeed for the same reason that I loved and still love *The Swiss Family Robinson*. I could lecture to you now on *The Swiss Family Robinson* and it would be a glowing lecture, because of the emotions felt in boyhood. When my brain decays entirely I shall not bother any more over great literature. I shall go back to the romantic shore where the "ship struck with a fearful shock," emitting four demigods named Fritz, Ernest, Jack and little Franz, together with their father, their mother, and a cushion, which contained all the appliances necessary for a ten years' residence in the tropics. That is my eternal summer, that is what *The Swiss Family Robinson* means to me, and is not it all that Sir Walter Scott means to some of you? Is he really more than a reminder of early happiness? And until our brains do decay, must not we put all this aside when we attempt to understand books?

In the second place, Scott's fame rests upon one genuine basis. He could tell a story.

So Mr. Forster writes, and then he proceeds to give in seven pages a long paraphrase, as he calls it, of the story of *The Antiquary*, in order to reveal his "simple devices" as a story teller. But nowhere does he express a word of admiration for the Scottish characters and talk of Edie Ochiltree and his various friends, of the Mucklebackits, of the Antiquary himself. The only quotations he gives in his seven pages of "paraphrase" are selected from Scott's conventional English prose. He is indeed so prejudiced against *The Antiquary* that he speaks of its "idiotic use of marriage as a finale"; that dictum, impartially applied, would make Jane Austen an idiot. What is sauce for the goose is sauce for the gander.

As to the alleged nursery origins of our love for Scott, *Rob Roy* was read to me when I was a child, but *The Antiquary* was not. My love of *The Antiquary* is wholly an adult passion. Mr. Forster will be glad to know that I also loved *The Swiss Family Robinson* when I was a small boy. A finer collection of wild animals from all the quarters of the globe is nowhere else to be found on one desert island. But for grown-up readers I do not place it on a level with *The Antiquary*.

Now the only way to put you in a position to judge between us in this matter, is to read you a fair specimen of the book.

At the beginning of chapter Thirty-four, the antiquary Mr. Oldbuck goes to condole with the old fisherman, Saunders Mucklebackit, whose favourite and only son Steenie has just been drowned out fishing with his father.

When he came in front of the fisherman's hut, he observed a man working intently, as if to repair a shattered boat which lay upon the beach, and, going up to him, was surprised to find it was Mucklebackit himself. "I am glad," he said, in a tone of sympathy —"I am glad, Saunders, that you feel yourself able to make this exertion."

"And what would ye have me to do," answered the fisher gruffly, "unless I wanted to see four children starve, because ane is drowned? It's weel wi' you gentles, that can sit in the house wi' handkerchers at your een when ye lose a friend; but the like o' us maun to our wark again, if our hearts were beating as hard as my hammer."

Without taking more notice of Oldbuck, he proceeded in his labour; and the Antiquary, to whom the display of human nature under the influence of agitating passions was never indifferent, stood beside him, in silent attention, as if watching the progress of the work. He observed more than once the man's hard features, as if by the force of association, prepare to accompany the sound of the saw and hammer with his usual symphony of a rude tune, hummed or whistled,—and as often a slight twitch of convulsive expression showed, that ere the sound was uttered, a cause for suppressing it rushed upon his mind. At length, when he had patched a considerable rent, and was beginning to mend another his feelings appeared altogether to derange the power of attention necessary for his work. The piece of wood which he was about to nail on was at first too long; then he sawed it off too short; then chose another equally ill adapted for the purpose. At length, throwing it down in anger, after wiping his dim eye with his quivering hand, he exclaimed, "There is a curse either on me or on this auld black bitch of a boat, that I have hauled up high and dry, and patched and clouted sae mony years, that she might drown my poor Steenie at the end of them, an' be d——d to her!" and he flung his hammer against the boat, as if she had been the intentional cause of his misfortune. Then recollecting himself, he added, "Yet what needs ane be angry at her, that has neither soul nor sense?—though I am no that muckle better mysell.

She's but a rickle o' auld rotten deals nailed thegither, and warped wi' the wind and the sea—and I am a dour carle, battered by foul weather at sea and land till I am maist as senseless as hersell. She maun be mended though again' the morning-tide—that's a thing o' necessity."

Thus speaking, he went to gather together his instruments and attempt to resume his labour,—but Oldbuck took him kindly by the arm. "Come, come," he said, "Saunders, there is no work for you this day—I'll send down Shavings the carpenter to mend the boat, and he may put the day's work into my account—and you had better not come out to-morrow, but stay to comfort your family under this dispensation, and the gardener will bring you some vegetables and meal from Monkbarns."

"I thank ye, Monkbarns," answered the poor fisher; "I am a plain-spoken man, and hae little to say for mysell; I might hae learned fairer fashions frae my mither lang syne, but I never saw muckle gude they did her; however, I thank ye. Ye were aye kind and neighbourly, whatever folk says o' your being near and close; and I hae often said in thae times when they were ganging to raise up the puir folk against the gentles—I hae often said, ne'er a man should steer a hair touching to Monkbarns while Steenie and I could wag a finger—and so said Steenie too. And, Monkbarns, when ye laid his head in the grave (and mony thanks for the respect), ye saw the mouls laid on an honest lad that likit you well, though he made little phrase about it."

Well, that is typical of Sir Walter, when his Scottish sock is on. Earlier in the same book occurs the story of the antiquary's discovery of what he takes for the ruins of a Roman Prætorium, when his dream is rudely shattered by the first words spoken by Edie Ochiltree, "Prætorian here, Prætorian there, I mind the biggin o't". The old beggar had built it himself. Now I find this scene much better, much more "in the round" than the similar story of "Bill Stumps his mark" in *Pickwick*. I do not say this in derogation of Dickens: I love *Pickwick* especially after Sam Weller has appeared. I am only reclaiming for Sir Walter his place among his peers.

Neither has Mr. Forster any use for *The Heart of Midlothian* (p. 17). It is, he says scornfully, "provincial", "a handful out of Edinburgh". Why not? As well out of Edinburgh as out of

Paris or London. Personally I prefer the provincial to the suburban. It has more salt in it. It is nearer to earth. The characters in Mr. Forster's own novels and short stories are essentially suburban, though often living abroad in foreign pensions or hotels. It is an uprooted society, not growing in any soil like Dandie Dinmont, Bailie Nicol Jarvie and the Deans family. Mr. Forster's descriptive power, poetic feeling and humour make his stories interesting, though sometimes by bringing in very "provincial" Italians or Indians. To my thinking the best of the many good scenes he has written, is the acting of the opera in the "provincial" theatre of Monteriano in *Where angels fear to tread*. The excellence of his novels is not on account of but in spite of the metropolitan and suburban triviality of the English society he depicts. There Sir Walter, in his Scottish novels, has the advantage of him.

Moreover in his essay on the poet Crabbe, in *Two Cheers for Democracy*—a first-rate piece of appreciative criticism—Mr. Forster uses these words about that exceedingly "provincial" author; Crabbe, he says, 'had the great good luck to belong to a particular part of England and to belong to it all his life'. He adds that Crabbe and Wordsworth 'had this in common,' 'that they were regional, and that their earliest impressions were the most durable'. Now if Crabbe, as Mr. Forster thinks, gained as an artist by being provincial and by carrying always in his mind's eye the image of the mud flats of the east coast and the memory of the pettifogging inhabitants of the Borough of Aldeburgh, why should he make it an offence in Scott that he also is "provincial" with all Scotland for his province? Edinburgh and its Eighteenth-century folk seem to me less "provincial" in any bad sense than Aldeburgh and its inhabitants as depicted in the Tales of Crabbe. Surely Scotland and the Scottish character is as fit a subject for imaginative art as Aldeburgh. I do not think Mr. Forster is consistent in this matter.

And in fact the inferior part of *The Heart of Midlothian* is by no means the "provincial" Jeanie Deans and her father, but the stagey hero-villain from south England. At any rate the "provincial" Jeanie Deans walks up from Edinburgh to London to beg the life of her sister Effie, who has been wrongfully condemned for child-murder. At the end of her heroic journey, Jeanie finds a powerful patron in the Duke of Argyle. He takes her to see Queen Caroline, George II's wife and political adviser. They find her in no gentle mood, enraged against the Scottish nation for the murder of Captain Porteous by the Edinburgh mob, and the public conspiracy to conceal the culprits.

"Well, my Lord," said her Majesty, "all these fine speeches do not convince me of the propriety of so soon showing any mark of favour to your—I suppose I must not say rebellious?—but, at least, your very disaffected and intractable metropolis. Why, the whole nation is in a league to screen the savage and abominable murderers of that unhappy man; otherwise, how is it possible but that, of so many perpetrators, and engaged in so public an action for such a length of time, one at least must have been recognised? Even this wench, for aught I can tell, may be a depository of the secret. Hark you, young woman, had you any friends engaged in the Porteous mob?"

"No, madam," answered Jeanie, happy that the question was so framed that she could, with a good conscience, answer it in the negative.

"But I suppose," continued the Queen, "if you were possessed of such a secret, you would hold it a matter of conscience to keep it to yourself?"

"I would pray to be directed and guided what was the line of duty, madam," answered Jeanie.

"Yes, and take that which suited your own inclinations," replied her Majesty.

"If it like you, madam," said Jeanie, "I would hae gaen to the end of the earth to save the life of John Porteous, or any other unhappy man of his condition; but I might lawfully doubt how far I am called upon to be the avenger of his blood, though it may become the civil magistrate to do so. He is dead and gane to his place, and they that have slain him must answer for their ain act. But my sister—my puir sister Effie, still lives, though her days and hours are numbered! She still lives, and a word of the King's mouth might restore her to a broken-hearted auld man, that never, in his daily and nightly exercise, forgot to pray that his Majesty might be blessed with a long and a prosperous reign, and that his throne, and the throne of his posterity, might be established in righteousness. O, madam, if ever ye ken'd what it was to sorrow for and with a sinning and a suffering creature, whose mind is sae tossed that she can be neither ca'd fit to live or die, have some compassion on our misery!—Save an honest house from dishonour, and an unhappy girl, not eighteen years of age, from an early and dreadful death! Alas! it is not when we sleep soft and wake merrily ourselves that we think on other people's sufferings. Our hearts are waxed light within us then, and we are for righting our ain wrangs and fighting our ain battles. But when the hour of trouble comes to the mind or to the body—and seldom may it visit your Leddyship—and when the hour of death comes, that comes to high and low—lang and late may it be yours!—O, my Leddy, then it isna what we hae dune for oursells, but what we hae dune for others that we think on maist pleasantly. And the thoughts that ye hae intervened to spare the puir thing's life will be sweeter in that hour, come when it may, than if a word of your mouth could hang the haill Porteous mob at the tail of ae tow."

"This is eloquence," said her Majesty to the Duke of Argyle.

Well, I agree with the Queen. But Mr. Forster tells us that Scott 'has a trivial mind and a heavy style. He cannot construct'. For my part I should have thought that what I have just read was neither trivial nor heavy nor ill constructed. In fact I regard Jeanie's appeal as a masterpiece of prose construction. And Meg Merrilies' curse was admired and analysed by Verrall precisely as a magnificent bit of prose construction:

"Ride your ways," said the gipsy, "ride your ways, Laird of Ellangowan—ride your ways, Godfrey Bertram!—This day have ye quenched seven smoking hearths—see if the fire in your ain parlour burn the blither for that. Ye have riven the thack off seven cottar houses—look if your ain roof-tree stand the faster.— Ye may stable your stirks in the shealings at Derncleugh—see that the hare does not couch on the hearthstane at Ellangowan.—Ride your ways, Godfrey Bertram—what do ye glower after our folk for?—There's thirty hearts there, that wad hae wanted bread ere ye had wanted sunkets, and spent their lifeblood ere ye had scratched your finger. Yes—there's thirty yonder, from the auld wife of an hundred to the babe that was born last week, that ye have turned out o' their bits o' bields, to sleep with the tod and the black-cock in the muirs!—Ride your ways, Ellangowan.—Our bairns are hinging at our weary backs—look that your braw cradle at hame be the fairer spread up—not that I am wishing ill to little Harry, or to the babe that's yet to be born—God forbid —and make them kind to the poor, and better folk than their father!—And now, ride e'en your ways; for these are the last words ye'll ever hear Meg Merrilies speak, and this is the last reise that I'll ever cut in the bonny woods of Ellangowan."

Well, if the passages I have quoted are trivial, heavy and ill constructed, as Mr. Forster says, may I be—never again allowed to read books!

Mr. Forster has indeed made a proper and a useful distinction between Scott's *historical importance*, which he fully admits, and Scott's *intrinsic value* to the reader of later times, which he thinks very small. It is on the latter point that I have stated my difference of view. Unlike Mr. Forster I see a great deal of high intrinsic value, but I confess that I cannot find much of it outside the novels of Scottish character: *Waverley*, *Rob Roy*, *Guy Mannering*, *Heart of Midlothian*, *Old Mortality*, *A Legend of Montrose* (or shall we rather call it *Sir Dugald Dalgetty*?), *Redgauntlet* (especially *Wandering Willie's Tale*) and that strangely-begotten dream of his sick-bed, *The Bride of Lammermuir*. The rest of Scott's novels seem to me of lesser intrinsic value, though some are much better than others.

But all his work, including of course the Lays which I am not discussing, had great historical importance; England and all Europe welcomed it with a roar of delight and surprise. Men had never before seen realism, romance and history thus welded together. It was a new birth of time. The historical consequences of its immense popularity were threefold.

(1) First, it put Scotland into the map for Englishmen, who had till then wallowed in ignorance and prejudice about North Britain.

(2) Secondly it founded the historical novel, and more

generally made a new era in fiction. That is a subject I leave to learned critics. I merely note it as a layman and pass on.

(3) Thirdly—and this is what concerns me as an historian—it altered men's way of regarding the past. The canvas of history, hitherto filled with abstractions and generalized types as in Gibbon, was filled in Scott's romances with flesh and blood human beings, differing one from another as individuals. History was seen as "a fair field full of *folk*". Moreover, Scott had written social history in his novels—as for instance his picture of the relations of Highlander and Lowlander in the Fifteenth and other chapters of *Waverley*. Before Scott had died, two young men, both of Scottish origin by the way, Macaulay and Carlyle, demanded that social history, as shown in Scott, should no longer be monopolized by the novelist but become a part of the historian's task. But I have dealt elsewhere with the effect of Scott's novels on history and will say no more of it here. (See my *Autobiography and other Essays*, pp. 200–5, essay on *The Influence of Sir Walter Scott on History*.)

Scott's best successor in his own line of business was Stevenson. His Scottish dialogues and characters in *Kidnapped*, *Catriona*, *Master of Ballantrae*, *Weir of Hermiston* and *The Merry Men* are as good as Scott's, and Stevenson had the wisdom and the talent to avoid the flatness of so much of Scott's narrative. He strove to load every rift with ore. Stevenson was an artist; Scott was a cross between a publisher's hack, an antiquarian and a creative genius of the first order of originality and performance. Scott fished the murex up; Stevenson brought up to date the method of manufacture.

VI

THIS is my last lecture. I want to speak first about George Meredith, particularly as a poet, and then make a few concluding remarks on the layman's relation to letters.

The reputation of George Meredith, both as novelist and as poet, has had many ups and downs. He was born in 1828 and died at the age of eighty. In 1862 he published one of the greatest of his poems, the sonnet sequence of *Modern Love*. It was virulently attacked by the principal reviews as "immoral", because its subject was an unhappy marriage, though its treatment of that prohibited theme was serious, tragic and moral. These critics might at least as well have attacked as immoral another still more famous sonnet sequence, and they would no doubt have done so if it had been "begotten" in their own time. But indeed I think we may say of the author of *Modern Love* what he himself said of Shakespeare:

> He probed from hell to hell
> Of human passions, but of love deflowered
> His wisdom was not.

Swinburne, enraged at the folly of the critics, rushed into the fray, declaring the greatness of *Modern Love* as "a poem above the aim and beyond the reach of any but its author". But it was no use. Meredith was a condemned man, and for long years only a few friends paid attention either to his novels or to his poems, though *Harry Richmond* came out in 1871, and the final version of *Love in the Valley* in 1878.

This attack on *Modern Love* is another case where as a layman I complain of the deeds of critics; at that time they were wrapped up, to the eyes and over, in the swaddling clothes of mid-Victorian prudery, but every age has its own forms of blindness. The utter neglect in which Meredith was left during the first and formative half of his life as an author, had an unfortunate influence on his work. Since neither the critics nor the public would listen to him, he soliloquized in prose and poetry, which became therefore increasingly eccentric and obscure. He once told me that as a young man he had hoped to be a popular novelist like Dickens, but soon found it to be impossible, and so wrote to please himself alone.

Recognition, though tardy, came at last. There were three distinct periods of the long Victorian age, and during the last of them, for twenty years before the Queen died, Meredith was regarded by a new and more enlightened generation of critics as an odd but a great man. Appreciation came first to his novels, on the publication of *The Egoist* in 1879. Its intellectual power and caprice, its humour and its psychology exactly suited the mental atmosphere of the 'eighties and 'nineties. For my part I love the first half of the novel, but he had not, to my thinking, the ability to tell a long tale strongly and clearly to the end. I am bored by much of the last part. I wish Mrs. Mountstuart Jenkinson had said "you see he has a leg", and then forever held her peace. Surely this great novel would have been even greater if Clara and her father, the Egoist, Crossjay and Vernon Whitford had been left more to themselves without so much intricate plot and so many minor characters of inferior conception.

The most vivid appreciation and criticism of *The Egoist* is the homage done to Meredith in Sir Max Beerbohm's *Christmas Garland*, perhaps the wittiest parody ever written.

Meredith, in my opinion, had more intellectual power and finesse, and stronger imagination than any other of the Victorians, but neither in his novels nor in his poetry did he know how to employ them perfectly—except, as I shall presently argue, in some of his poems.

To my mind, *Harry Richmond* is the greatest of his novels. It is somewhat fantastic; the leading characters, all except the hero who is mere cork on the torrent, are a bit above the size of life, especially that most remarkable of all his creations Harry Richmond's father, and his opposite the Squire; the incidents might each of them conceivably have occurred, but their sum total leaves a taste of slight improbability. The living statue on the promontory is certainly more unusual than anything that takes place in the towns of Middlemarch or Barchester. The general effect is that of very exciting people in an exciting world, a trifle more highly raised than reality. This may be a fault, but if you can put yourself in the mood it lifts the spirit high. His women, indeed, are more often on the real level of life, drawn sympathetically and from within: Clara Middleton, Diana and her friend Emma, Ottilia and Janet, Rose and Renée. In those days intelligent women were grateful to Meredith, and with reason, for he fought their battle.

His intellectual agility and finesse are very great, but they often lead him into a bog: his poetical imagination never. For me, the best scenes in the novels are the most poetical, especially where the human situation is set in some aspect of nature: the crisis in the boat at sea under the Venetian Alps in chapter IX of *Beauchamp*, Vernon Whitford under the cherry tree, Diana's walk at dawn upon the mountain side above Lugano—and a hundred more. His novels, no less than Hardy's, are the novels of a poet.

Before I pass on to consider his poems, I will mention one thing by the way. Severe critic as he was of England, in her relations to Ireland and much else, he valued her for her real qualities and for her service to the world. If she fell, he wrote, "mankind would breathe a harsher air". Well, she has not fallen, but she has relatively declined, and the air is already more harsh. Meredith had received part of his schooling in Germany just before the era of Bismarck, and from the boyish experience he sensed much of the future. Already before 1870 he knew that the Germans would be our rivals, and dangerous rivals too, because they educated their people, which we then did not; because they made long plans and carried them through; and obeyed military rulers who believed in force. His mingled admiration and fear of the Germans comes out in *Harry Richmond*, and the German chapters of it are well worth comparing with the very similar warning issued in the

same year 1871 by Matthew Arnold in his *Friendship's Garland*.
Though he was an advanced Liberal in other matters, Meredith
believed that universal military service would prove the only
means of preserving our island, anchored off a continent to
whose real forces and tendencies we were shutting our eyes.
As early as 1891 he had written *England before the Storm*.

> The day that is the night of days,
> With cannon-fire for sun ablaze,
> We spy from any billow's lift;
> And England still this tidal drift!
> Would she to sainted forethought vow
> A space before the thunders flood,
> That martyr of its hour might now
> Spare her the tears of blood.
>
> Asleep upon her ancient deeds,
> She hugs the vision plethora breeds,
> And counts her manifold increase
> Of treasure in the fruits of peace.
> What curse on earth's improvident,
> When the dread trumpet shatters rest,
> Is wreaked, she knows, yet smiles content
> As cradle rocked from breast.
>
> She, impious to the Lord of Hosts,
> The valour of her offspring boasts,
> Mindless that now on land and main
> His heeded prayer is active brain.
> No more great heart may guard the home,
> Save eyed and armed and skilled to cleave
> Yon swallower wave with shroud of foam,
> We see not distant heave.
>
> They stand to be her sacrifice,
> The sons this mother flings like dice,
> To face the odds and brave the Fates;
> As in those days of starry dates,
> When cannon cannon's counterblast
> Awakened, muzzle muzzle bowled,
> And high in swathe of smoke the mast
> Its fighting rag outrolled.

Recognition of Meredith as a poet followed slowly after his recognition as a novelist, partly because the new poems that he published in the 'eighties and 'nineties were many of them difficult and obscure, too heavily weighted with thought and imagery imperfectly digested, to be readable by ordinary mortals. But they became the study of the young intellectuals of the day, among whom, strange as it may seem to you, was numbered the hoary old Philistine who is now addressing you. I often visited Meredith at Box Hill, and in 1906 I published a book called *The Poetry and Philosophy of George Meredith*. It went through several editions and then died. *Requiescat in pace*. It served my generation but it would not serve yours. It was largely concerned with Meredith's poetical philosophy, his reading of Earth, in which he was more interested than in Heaven. But ideas date, while art survives. It is as a poet, not as a poetical philosopher, that he has claim to immortality. I was also permitted to edit and publish in 1912 his collected Poetical Works, to which I added some explanatory notes. My work may or may not have been well done, but in any case it is a disaster that his collected poems are now out of print.

In the last few years of his life, Meredith was regarded by many as the head of English letters. In 1898 Leslie Stephen forwarded to him a parchment bearing the good wishes of the authors of the day on his seventieth birthday, and ten years later his eightieth birthday was celebrated with even fuller honours. His friendly rival, Hardy, was generous in his praise, and wrote a beautiful poem on his death in 1909.

By that time much of his poetry was widely known and admired. Then came the First World War, and when we emerged from it his work in verse and prose no longer appealed to the new generation. He had sunk once more below the capricious horizon of literary fashion. But I rejoice to see that in our own latest age two of our poet-critics do full justice to his poetic powers. I commend to you Mr. Siegfried Sassoon's *Meredith* (1948) and Mr. Day Lewis's edition of *Modern Love* of the same year with an introduction that leaves unsaid nothing

that I would wish to say. After briefly telling the story of
Modern Love, Mr. Day Lewis writes:

> Such a summary gives little idea of the poem's dramatic move-
> ment, its skilful alternations of crisis with calm, tragic necessity
> with lyrical illusion, cynicism or despair with faith and tender-
> ness; nor of Meredith's quite extraordinary psychological insight;
> nor of the technical mastery which enabled him both to transmute
> psychology into poetry and to make the meditative sonnet form
> appear a perfectly apt vehicle for a passionate monodrama.

Mr. Day Lewis has also said some very interesting things about
Meredith's use of the poetic image, in his well-known Clark
Lectures on that subject. Well, here is an instance of an image
from *Modern Love*:

> They say, that Pity in Love's service dwells
> A porter at the rosy temple's gate.
> I missed him going: but it is my fate
> To come upon him now beside his wells;
> Whereby I know that I Love's temple leave,
> And that the purple doors have closed behind.

As I feel that Mr. Day Lewis has placed the merits of *Modern
Love* before the present generation much better than I can do,
I will only enforce the argument by quoting the Sixteenth
sonnet and the Fiftieth, the last of all.

In the Sixteenth sonnet, the husband recalls a moment from
their happier past, now full of tragic significance:

> In our old shipwrecked days there was an hour,
> When in the firelight steadily aglow,
> Joined slackly, we beheld the red chasm grow
> Among the clicking coals. Our library-bower
> That eve was left to us: and hushed we sat
> As lovers to whom Time is whispering.
> From sudden-opened doors we heard them sing;
> The nodding elders mixed good wine with chat.
> Well knew we that Life's greatest treasure lay
> With us, and of it was our talk. "Ah yes!
> Love dies!" I said: I never thought it less.
> She yearned to me that sentence to unsay.

> Then when the fire domed blackening, I found
> Her cheek was salt against my kiss, and swift
> Up the sharp scale of sobs her breast did lift:—
> Now am I haunted by that taste! that sound!

The last sonnet of the series, after the wife's suicide, has en-
riched our language with some phrases often quoted by people
who do not even know that they are Meredith's:

> Thus piteously Love closed what he begat:
> The union of this ever-diverse pair!
> These two were rapid falcons in a snare,
> Condemned to do the flitting of the bat.
> Lovers beneath the singing sky of May,
> They wandered once; clear as the dew on flowers:
> But they fed not on the advancing hours:
> Their hearts held cravings for the buried day.
> Then each applied to each that fatal knife,
> Deep questioning, which probes to endless dole.
> Ah, what a dusty answer gets the soul
> When hot for certainties in this our life!—
> In tragic hints here see what evermore
> Moves dark as yonder midnight ocean's force,
> Thundering like ramping hosts of warrior horse,
> To throw that faint thin line upon the shore!

The poem of Meredith's which first won the affection of an
appreciable number of readers, was of course *Love in the Valley*.
I remember that when I used to tell my friends, half a century
ago, that Meredith was a poet as well as a novelist, one of them
replied, "O yes, he wrote *Love in the Valley*; one need not read
anything else". It is a poem of young love, set in the south
English countryside, following round the farmer's year from
the coming of one spring to the next. To my thinking it is the
most beautiful love poem of that length to be found in our
language. The first version of it, for which I should certainly
not advance any such claim, was published in 1851, when he
was twenty-three years old, and still happily married to
Peacock's daughter. Seven years later she ran away from him.
After that terrible experience, he wrote *Modern Love*; the

relation of that poem to the actual facts of his broken marriage has been treated by Mr. Day Lewis in his Introduction, in a way on which I cannot improve. Then more years passed, and Meredith, at the height of his poetic powers, took up the first version of *Love in the Valley*, which had the wonderful lilting metre, and some beautiful lines, but was full also of juvenile weaknesses, some almost puerile. Out of this beginning, he produced as a middle-aged man the *Love in the Valley* that we now have. He changed the weak words and lines to strength or replaced them altogether. And he more than doubled the length of the poem. Yet it has not lost the freshness of the dawn of young love when it is bliss to be alive, though a strain of deeper poetry has been added to that theme. It is almost impossible to choose out of the twenty-six stanzas any that are more beautiful than the rest. The only charge that could be made against the poem is monotony of feeling and beauty—whereas *Modern Love* is distinguished for the variety of its moods.

I know few things more interesting than the way in which this early love poem of an enamoured boy was changed by its author, twenty-five years later, from weakness to strength.

Here is the stanza about dawn as it stood in the early version of 1851:

> Happy, happy time, when the grey star twinkles
> Over the fields all fresh with bloomy dew;
> When the cold-cheek'd dawn grows ruddy up the twilight,
> And the gold sun wakes, and weds her in the blue,
> Then when my darling tempts the early breezes
> She the only star that dies not with the dark!
> Powerless to speak all the ardour of my passion
> I catch her little hand as we listen to the lark.

Here is the stanza that takes its place in the final version of 1878:

> Happy, happy time, when the white star hovers
> Low over dim fields fresh with bloomy dew,
> Near the face of dawn, that draws athwart the darkness,
> Threading it with colour, like yewberries the yew.

Thicker crowd the shades as the grave East deepens
  Glowing, and with crimson a long cloud swells.
Maiden still the morn is; and strange she is, and secret;
  Strange her eyes; her cheeks are cold as cold sea-shells.

So too the last stanza of the version of 1851 has been replaced
by a much stronger ending to the poem. As, I am sorry to say,
Love in the Valley is out of print and can only be obtained
second-hand, I make no apology for reading you four more
stanzas, taken at random, for all the stanzas in the poem are
as good one as another.

Lovely are the curves of the white owl sweeping
  Wavy in the dusk lit by one large star.
Lone on the fir-branch, his rattle-note unvaried,
  Brooding o'er the gloom, spins the brown eve-jar.
Darker grows the valley, more and more forgetting:
  So were it with me if forgetting could be willed.
Tell the grassy hollow that holds the bubbling well-spring,
  Tell it to forget the source that keeps it filled.

All the girls are out with their baskets for the primrose;
  Up lanes, woods through, they troop in joyful bands.
My sweet leads: she knows not why, but now she loiters,
  Eyes the bent anemones, and hangs her hands.
Such a look will tell that the violets are peeping,
  Coming the rose: and unaware a cry
Springs in her bosom for odours and for colour,
  Covert and the nightingale; she knows not why.

Front door and back of the mossed old farmhouse
  Open with the morn, and in a breezy link
Freshly sparkles garden to stripe-shadowed orchard,
  Green across a rill where on sand the minnows wink.
Busy in the grass the early sun of summer
  Swarms, and the blackbird's mellow fluting notes
Call my darling up with round and roguish challenge:
  Quaintest, richest carol of all the singing throats!

Doves of the fir-wood walling high our red roof
  Through the long noon coo, crooning through the coo.
Loose droop the leaves, and down the sleepy roadway
  Sometimes pipes a chaffinch; loose droops the blue.

Cows flap a slow tail knee-deep in the river,
    Breathless, given up to sun and gnat and fly.
Nowhere is she seen; and if I see her nowhere,
    Lightning may come, straight rains and tiger sky.

In *Love in the Valley* the purely human emotion is exalted by the lover's contact with the beauties of Nature, and his sense of Nature's underlying strength akin to mankind. Meredith's philosophy of Earth was based on the fact that we are literally her children. Sometimes he states this philosophy of our kinship with earth too intellectually, but often it is an unconscious but intrinsic element in his best poems such as: *Earth and wedded Woman*, *Juggling Jerry*, *The Thrush in February*, *Melampus*, *The Orchard and the Heath*, *The Spirit of Earth in Autumn*, *Phoebus with Admetus*, *The Day of the Daughter of Hades*, and many more.

There is indeed a rich abundance and variety, more than enough to establish his high place among our poets. It is true that his best poems are interspersed with others of a forbidding obscurity of diction—written as I have said to please himself rather than the public. The grammar is often syncopated and abstruse; images and half images are hurled one on another in bewildering confusion—as for instance in *The Sage Enamoured*, *The Empty Purse* and the more famous *Woods of Westermain*. In the days when I struggled with these obscurities I found in them much more buried treasure than in the banality of Wordsworth's later poetry, which occupies as large a proportion of his Collected Works as the obscure occupies in those of Meredith. We must judge all poets by their *best* work.

Many of our poets have celebrated the song of the lark and the song of the nightingale. Here is Meredith's contribution. First, in *The Lark Ascending*:

        He rises and begins to round,
        He drops the silver chain of sound,
        Of many links without a break,
        In chirrup, whistle, slur and shake,
        All intervolved and spreading wide,
        Like water-dimples down a tide

Where ripple ripple overcurls
And eddy into eddy whirls;
A press of hurried notes that run
So fleet they scarce are more than one,
Yet changeingly the trills repeat
And linger ringing while they fleet,
Sweet to the quick o' the ear, and dear
To her beyond the handmaid ear,
Who sits beside our inner springs,
Too often dry for this he brings,
Which seems the very jet of earth
At sight of sun, her music's mirth,
As up he wings the spiral stair,
A song of light, and pierces air
With fountain ardour, fountain play,
To reach the shining tops of day,
And drink in everything discerned
An ecstasy to music turned.

    *   *   *

And such the water-spirit's chime
On mountain heights in morning's prime,
Too freshly sweet to seem excess,
Too animate to need a stress;
But wider over many heads
The starry voice ascending spreads,
Awakening, as it waxes thin,
The best in us to him akin;
And every face to watch him raised
Puts on the light of children praised.

Then take from *Night of Frost in May*, this description of the
nightingale's song, first faintly heard, from a single throat, then
loudly multiplied:

In this shrill hush of quietude,
The ear conceived a severing cry.
Almost it let the sound elude,
When chuckles three, a warble shy,
From hazels of the garden came,
Near by the crimson-windowed farm.
They laid the trance on breath and frame,
A prelude of the passion-charm.

> Then soon was heard, not sooner heard
> Than answered, doubled, trebled, more,
> Voice of an Eden in the bird
> Renewing with his pipe of four
> The sob: a troubled Eden, rich
> In throb of heart; unnumbered throats
> Flung upward at a fountain's pitch
> The fervour of the four long notes,
> That on the fountain's pool subside,
> Exult and ruffle and upspring:
> Endless the crossing multiplied
> Of silver and of golden string,
> There chimed a bubbled underbrew
> With witch-wild spray of vocal dew.

Chaucer, Milton, Wordsworth, Keats have written noble lines
in praise of the nightingale's song, and of its historic symbolism
to men. But this of Meredith's is not merely praise of the song;
it represents the song itself. It is the most accurate description
of what we hear when we listen to the nightingale, and of its
emotional effect upon our poetic nerve.

Meredith is poet of out of doors, by night and by day. He
spent much of his best years, before illness imprisoned his old
age, in long cross-country walks and in communion with
woods, fields and hills, with sun, wind and stars.

> I, who love old hymning night
> And know the dryad voices well.

> I know him, February's thrush,
> And loud at eve he valentines.

> Now the North-wind ceases
> The warm South-west awakes;
> Swift fly the fleeces,
> Thick the blossom flakes.

Yet some of his poems are historical, like the famous *Nuptials
of Attila*. One group, entitled *Odes in Contribution to the Song of
French History*, illustrates the strength and weakness of his verse
and their relation to each other in time, the gradual growth

of the habit of obscurity. Meredith loved France while he respected and feared Germany. Of both, as also of England, he was a most discerning critic. Of the four Odes on French History, the first in order of composition is by far the best: it is called *France, December 1870*, and it was actually published in 1871, while the German armies were overrunning prostrate France.

> We look for her that sunlike stood
> Upon the forehead of our day,
> An orb of nations, radiating food
> For body and for mind alway.
> Where is the Shape of glad array;
> The nervous hands, the front of steel,
> The clarion tongue? Where is the bold proud face?
> We see a vacant place;
> We hear an iron heel.
>
> O she that made the brave appeal
> For manhood when our time was dark,
> And from our fetters drove the spark
> Which was as lightning to reveal
> New seasons, with the swifter play
> Of pulses, and beniger day;
> She that divinely shook the dead
> From living man; that stretched ahead
> Her resolute forefinger straight,
> And marched toward the gloomy gate
> Of earth's Untried, gave note, and in
> The good name of Humanity
> Called forth the daring vision! she,
> She likewise half corrupt of sin,
> Angel and Wanton! can it be?
> Her star has foundered in eclipse,
> The shriek of madness on her lips;
> Shreds of her, and no more, we see.
> There is horrible convulsion, smothered din,
> As of one that in a grave-cloth struggles to be free.

The Ode is true poetry and yet it is also a just comment on public events in their historical setting. At one point he goes

back to the conquests, triumphs, spoils of the Revolutionary
and Napoleonic armies, of which, as he thinks, the full retribu-
tion has only now in 1870 fallen on France.

> Ah, what a dawn of splendour, when her sowers
> Went forth and bent the necks of populations
> And of their terrors and humiliations
> Wove her the starry wreath that earthward lowers
> Now in the figure of a burning yoke!
> Her legions traversed North and South and East,
> Of Triumph they enjoyed the glutton's feast:
> They grafted the green sprig, they lopped the oak.
> They caught by the beard the tempests, by the scalp
> The icy precipices, and clove sheer through
> The heart of horror of the pinnacled Alp,
> Emerging not as men whom mortals knew.
>
> *   *   *
>
> . . . Yet, how they sucked the teats
> Of Carnage, thirsty issue of their dam,
> Whose eagles, angrier than their oriflamme,
> Flushed the vext earth with blood, green earth forgets.
> The gay young generations mask her grief;
> Where bled her children hangs the loaded sheaf.
> Forgetful is green earth; the Gods alone
> Remember everlastingly: they strike
> Remorselessly, and ever like for like.
> By their great memories the Gods are known.

I am sorry that this fine and perfectly intelligible poem,
France, December 1870, has been buried among the three other
Odes of French History (*The Revolution, Napoleon* and *Alsace-
Lorraine*) which are more than twenty years later in date of
composition and proportionately more difficult to read. They
are indeed a just and penetrating view of history, based on his
eager study in old age of the works of Albert Sorel and Vandal;
I have tried to make the historical meaning clear in the notes
I appended to his collected Poetical Works. But alas that
poetry should need to be elucidated! Yes, these Odes are
difficult. But the opening of the poem on Napoleon, that at
least speaks for itself:

> Cannon his name,
> Cannon his voice, he came.
> Who heard of him heard shaken hills,
> An earth at quake, to quiet stamped;
> Who looked on him beheld the will of wills,
> The driver of wild flocks where lions ramped.

One of the merits of Meredith's poems is their great variety, in theme, in mood, in metre. The strong, crude lines on Napoleon which I have just read, or the *Nuptials of Attila*, are in marked contrast to other poems I have quoted to you, or again to *Phoebus with Admetus* or the sonnets on *Lucifer in Starlight* and *The Star Sirius*, or the little lyrics of nature like

> Sweet as Eden is the air,
> And Eden-sweet the ray.
> No Paradise is lost for them
> Who foot by branching root and stem,
> And lightly with the woodland share
> The change of night and day.

Equally different is that unique *Hymn to Colour*, a poem difficult indeed, but rather for the mysticism of the feeling than for the over-intellectual character of the thought which militates against the poetic effect of much of his other work.

A dualism runs through the imagery of the *Hymn to Colour*. Light, Darkness and Colour answer to Life, Death and Love. Colour is to Light and Darkness as Love is to Life and Death. The poet, walking between Death and Life, is met by Love in the pale "land of dawn", between night and day, where dreams are floating fast to wreck on daylight.

> With Life and Death I walked when Love appeared,
> And made them on each side a shadow seem.
> Through wooded vales the land of dawn we neared,
> Where down smooth rapids whirls the helmless dream
> To fall on daylight; and night puts away
> Her darker veil for grey.

Then the sky lights up with the colours of dawn

> Look now where Colour, the soul's bridegroom, makes
> The house of heaven splendid for the bride.

The moments of Colour are fleeting, but they live for ever in memory, and so it is with the supreme moments of Love:

> Love eyed his rosy memories; he sang:
> O Bloom of dawn, breathed up from the gold sheaf
> Held springing beneath Orient! that dost hang
> The space of dewdrops running over leaf;
> Thy fleetingness is bigger in the ghost
> Than Time with all his host!
>
> Of thee to say behold, has said adieu:
> But love remembers how the sky was green,
> And how the grasses glimmered lightest blue;
> How saint-like grey took fervour: how the screen
> Of cloud grew violet; how thy moment came
> Between a blush and flame.
>
> They do not look through love to look on thee
> Grave heavenliness! nor know they joy of sight,
> Who deem the wave of rapt desire must be
> Its wrecking and last issue of delight.
> Dead seasons quicken in one petal-spot
> Of colour unforgot.

The tragedy is that Meredith's poems are out of print. I believe that *Modern Love*, in Mr. Day Lewis's edition, is the only one that can be bought first-hand. This should be remedied.

I should like now to end these lectures by a few last words, spoken as a layman to my brother readers of English literature.

The greatest, but not the best of the Masters of Trinity had a favourite maxim that "no man was ever written out of reputation but by himself". (Monk's *Bentley*, ed. 1833, I, p. 118.) Like most epigrams it is about half true. But of Bentley himself it is true without qualification. Christ Church mobilized the whole force of its wit (which was great) and of its Greek scholarship (which in those long-gone days was small) in a joint gigantic effort to debunk Bentley, or, to use his own more dignified language, to "write him out of reputation". Swift lent the powerful aid of his mockery to the assault. For a while the fashionable world thought that the wits had laughed the Cambridge pedant out of court. But the sequel was very different. It established Bentley's reputation for ever. For his reply to his antagonists on the question at issue, the *Letters of Phalaris*, was of quality so supreme as to become the starting point of a new era in mankind's conception of the Greek world. Having thus trampled his assailants under his feet, and erected over their prostrate bodies a monument of new knowledge, Bentley then proceeded, over a number of years, slightly to lower his own immense reputation by some of his later publications. More particularly in his edition of Milton he displayed scholarship indeed but a want of poetic feeling, ear and appreciation amazing in any sane man, a want that must have been a weakness to him as a textual critic, as I have been told is here and there discernible in his emendations of Horace. As to his Milton, "O that mine enemy had written a book!"— and he had many enemies. Yes, Bentley's own life illustrated to perfection the truth latent in his manly saying "No one was ever written out of reputation but by himself".

Nevertheless the maxim does not always apply. Take the case of another great classical scholar of the same College, a hundred years later, Porson. His famous *Letters to Archdeacon Travis* utterly and for ever destroyed the reputation of his antagonist. You may of course argue that Travis in a sense wrote himself out of reputation by adopting an impossible thesis. But had it not been for Porson's attack, most clergymen would have continued for long years to believe in the authenticity of the text of the Three Witnesses. By the way, I hope that those of you who have enough scholarship will not fail to read and enjoy Bentley's *Phalaris* (which rivalled Christ Church in wit as well as surpassed it in scholarship) and Porson's *Letters to Travis*, for they are jewels in the coronal of our English literature. Or at the very least read Monk's *Life of Bentley*, one of our great and truly readable biographies, which it ill becomes a Cambridge man not to know and love. To enjoy it, you need not know any Greek at all. Monk's *Bentley* is on the same sort of pleasure-giving level as Lockhart's *Scott* and my father's *Macaulay*.

But when we move from the realm of scholarship to the realm of pure letters, this saying of Bentley's tends to be rather less true. It is indeed difficult to debunk a scholar if he is right and you are wrong. For scholarship is a provable thing. But whether a poet or novelist is good or bad is a matter of opinion. No doubt the truth is known in heaven, in the perfect witness of all-judging Jove. But here on earth it is perfectly possible to write a good poet or novelist out of reputation, with great success at least for a period. Indeed it is often done.

For example, there was the famous debunking of Trollope. The bright young artists and writers of the eighteen-nineties, who produced the *Yellow Book* and much else of value, were very definitely a clique with ideals and shibboleths of their own, mainly drawn from Paris. A living picture of them and their ways of thought will be found in the first story of Sir Max Beerbohm's *Seven Men—Enoch Soames*, surely one of the best short stories in the world. Their shibboleths were art for art's sake, Flaubert and the meticulous search for the *juste mot*. Now it chanced that Trollope, who was certainly the most popular and perhaps the most highly esteemed novelist of the age, had recently died, bequeathing to the world an Autobiography in which he described how he had written his novels, not by inspiration and absinthe like an artist on the *rive gauche*, but like a British householder working on system, producing so many words a day at stated hours in the intervals of his work as a civil servant; and he made things worse by adding a list of his novels with the amount of money he had received for each of them. If this was to be tolerated, what became of art for art's sake and the patient search for the *juste mot*? One must in fairness recognize the dilemma in which the young men found themselves. They must either modify their theories or debunk Trollope. So he was cast out of the literary synagogue, labelled as that odious thing a *bourgeois*. It always seems to me odd that in literary as well as in political circles the word bourgeois has been used as a word of abuse, considering that almost all our great writers, beginning with Shakespeare and Milton were bourgeois in origin and upbringing, except only Shelley and Byron who were aristocrats. If the work of our bourgeois, in life and letters, were subtracted from England's achievement, we should be poor indeed. Now that economic and political circumstances are rapidly finishing off what is left of the independence of the English middle and professional classes, posterity will perhaps soon be able to judge for itself how much literature has gained by the disappearance of the hated bourgeois. However that may be, Trollope was most undeniably a bourgeois and had to be debunked. The operation was carried out successfully. But he has since revived. The volume of the *Dictionary of National Biography* that dealt with Trollope, published in the year 1899, contained the following remarkable admission and still more remarkable prophecy: 'His works may fall into temporary oblivion, but when the twentieth century desires to estimate the nineteenth, they will be disinterred and studied with an attention accorded to no contemporary work of the kind, except, perhaps George Eliot's Middlemarch.' For my part I was an enthusiastic inhabitant of Barchester before the debunking order was issued, while it was still operative and after its writ ceased to run. No set of men, young or old, clever or stupid, would ever have persuaded me that Mr. Crawley in the *Last Chronicle of Barset* is not one of the great characters of fiction. So you see these wholesale condemnations of writers who have been for many years admired by competent literary opinion are not always right, or even final. The fashion of the hour, even of the latest hour, will change some day, and is moreover quite as likely to be wrong as the fashion of earlier times.

It seems to me that the function of those who set the tone to literary opinion, whether professional critics or reviewers, is not to destroy wholesale long-established reputations, say of Scott, Trollope or Kipling, not to discourage young men from looking in certain famous authors for themselves, but rather to help them to distinguish between what is the strength and what is the weakness of each author, and above all to help readers in the very difficult task of finding out which are the best poems (or novels) of an author, for they are so often deeply buried in inferior work. The positive side of criticism is more important than the negative. It is the love of great poetry and good prose that we want to instil into the young. It is our greatest national inheritance and how little use we make of it.

But my last words in this course of lectures as a layman loving letters, shall be addressed not to the professional critics but to my brother laymen. In the long run it all rests on you readers. You and no one else can work out your own individual salvation. Read our great authors assiduously, not regardless of advice, but quite regardless of prohibitions, till you find out, each for yourself, what appeals to you. It is an individual matter; Jones will be moved by one author, Smith by another. For literature, poetry in particular but good prose only to a less degree, appeals through the ear to the heart; by sound and melody and the happy use of words it touches the inmost soul in each of us. That is how great poetry works if it works at all. It is not a set of intellectual conundrums, to be solved by certain rules. It is joy, joy in our inmost heart. It is a passion like love or it is nothing. One's passion for a poem often lasts all one's life. But sometimes, as one's experience and one's powers of mind increase, some of one's loves fall away or at least diminish, while others increase. Mature age will retain some of the same affections in poetry as youth, but not all. But do not bother about maturity while you are young. Wait till it comes; it will come soon enough. While you are young and all the poets are around you waiting to be read, find out what you can love, seeking joy in the springtime, and love it. It is your affair, and not the affair of anyone else at all. What an immense and variegated landscape is stretched around you for your delight. It is all free for you to search, of infinite variety in its appeal, from comic prose to the highest poetry, all the ages of England and all the moods of her most remarkable men set down in words inspired. It is all of it your heritage. Search it and enjoy it. It has been to me a great part of the value of life, and may it be the same to you.